FOODCRAFT

NERYS PURCHON was born in the 1930s in the small village of Llanddulas in North Wales, and even as a child she knew the name and use of each root, seed, plant and berry growing in the mountains — as she said, she comes "from a long line of witches"! Growing up in the country also made her familiar from an early age with the traditional culinary arts which result in a well-stocked larder.

Nerys then trained and practised as a nurse before she left the profession to raise five children.

She emigrated to Western Australia in 1968, took up a small farm near Bunbury which developed into a herb-growing business, and began to treat people who had physical and emotional problems. She next set up Rivendell Farm, Skin and Hair Products, which she later sold and established the Prancing Pony Restaurant.

Nerys and her husband now live in the town of Bunbury where she runs courses in meditation, stress management, herbalism and wholefood cookery. She is the author of the successful *Herbcraft: The Cultivation and Use of Herbs*.

This book is dedicated with love to my sister,
Joan

FOODCRAFT

GIFT FOOD FOR GOURMETS

by Nerys Purchon

illustrations by Dhenu Jennifer Clary
photographs by Michael Hemmings

Hodder & Stoughton
SYDNEY AUCKLAND LONDON TORONTO

I would like to thank the following people for their help so generously given:
Dhenu Clary for her lovely drawings and Michael Hemmings for the
stunning photographs.
Gill and John Banks and Liz and Lloyd Horne for allowing their homes to
be used for the photographs.
Jenny and Priya for inspiration and help with packaging and Yatra for
proofreading.
As always, thank you Prakash for your tolerance, help and understanding.

First published in 1991
by Hodder & Stoughton (Australia) Pty Limited
ACN 000 884855
10–16 South Street, Rydalmere, NSW, 2116.

National Library of Australia Cataloguing-in-Publication entry

   Purchon, Nerys.
      Foodcraft.

      Includes index.
      ISBN 0 340 53605 5 (hdbk)
      ISBN 0 340 54954 8 (pbk)

      1. Cookery. 2. Gifts. I. Title.

   641.5

Typeset in 10pt Stymie by G.T. Setters Pty Limited, Kenthurst
Printed by Colorcraft Ltd, Hong Kong

Contents

Introduction

This book is as much a 'Storeroom' recipe book as it is a food gift book. It is very comforting to open your larder door and see rows of gleaming, richly coloured jars and bottles. This is very important to me. It may be because I am a Taurean and love food, or it may be because I grew up during World War II when food was in very short supply and my mother preserved all surplus fruits and vegetables as a hedge against hunger.

There is something very special about making and sharing food: it makes us feel warm, loved and secure. What better feelings could any gift produce?

I am sure that at some time you have been faced with buying a present for someone who 'has everything' because they indulge every whim or because their desires are very simple. Another drama is the birthday or anniversary which you have forgotten! Your storeroom is the answer to these problems, as the 'instant' gift is just as far away as your larder. Not only does this book have recipes but it also gives ideas for the packaging, labelling and presentation of the gifts.

The visual presentation of a gift is as important as the presentation of food. Our mouths begin to water when we see beautifully prepared and presented food, and our minds begin to race with anticipation when we are given exciting looking packages.

The main focus on presentation in this book is on the baskets and their contents, but the gifts need not only be in baskets. Consider a back pack or school bag for a teenager, a mixing bowl for a cook, a casserole with the ingredients and recipe inside, and so on.

The gift baskets can be of any size. This will depend on the number of items you include and how much money you wish to spend. If you want to make a lavish gift you can include other items. These could be a beautiful cup and saucer in the 'tea time' basket, one or two interesting kitchen gadgets for the 'gourmet cook' basket, a checked tablecloth and some unbreakable plates and mugs for the picnic basket, or a special glass for the wine or liqueur connoisseur's basket. The baskets may be highly personalised, making them a pleasure to make and a delight to receive.

The layout of the recipes in this book may be unfamiliar to you. I have been using this method for many years, both when I owned a restaurant and when I run cooking classes. The students quickly become converts, as the layout leaves no room for errors and is very simple to use.

The recipes are read along the line instead of down the page, and each stage is separated by a rule. I show a sample below. The chicken livers are the first ingredient to be dealt with, after this is done you move to the next block and cook the onions. The last block tells you to add more ingredients and process all together.

CHICKEN LIVER PÂTÉ WITH COINTREAU

chicken livers	*500 g (1 lb)*	Wash well. Trim any skin or fat, and chop.
butter onion, diced	*¼ cup* *1 cup*	Sauté together until onion is soft. Add livers and cook until the livers change colour. Do not overcook.
black olives, stoned paprika fresh lemon thyme, chopped salt black pepper Cointreau or brandy	*4* *½ teaspoon* *½ teaspoon* *½ teaspoon* *½ teaspoon* *1 tablespoon*	Blend with liver mixture until smooth. Pack in dishes. To proceed, see opening remarks on pâtés (p.28).

If you first lay out all the ingredients (on the left-hand side of the recipe) in the order in which they will be used, then start with the preliminary instructions (if any) and move on to the blocks, you will find every recipe very quick and easy to follow.

Methods and Equipment

If you have few standards and no patience for details, better send out for pizza.
—Tom Wicker (b.1926)

Bruising Bruising allows flavour to escape but keeps the root or seed intact. Use a mortar and pestle (or similar bowl and heavy weight) to tap the root or seed enough to break the skin and flatten slightly but not to crush.

Cakes To test if cooked, gently push a skewer into the centre of the cake. If the cake is cooked, the skewer will come out dry. A cake which is not quite cooked 'sings'. As long as there is this sound, the centre of the cake is still moist.

Cheesecloth bags *See* **Jelly bags** below.

Chilli The oil in chillies can burn very badly. I keep a special little board for their preparation, to avoid accidents. It is best to wear rubber gloves and wash everything thoroughly *immediately* after use. If I seem to be over-emphatic I should tell you that I once rubbed one of my eyes while dealing with fresh chilli and I was in terrible pain for a day or so afterwards.

Chocolate To melt chocolate you will need a **double boiler** (see below). It is important that no steam or drops of water can reach the chcolate or it will 'seize' into an unworkable mess. The chocolate should be broken into very small pieces or be grated, before putting in the top pan. The water in the bottom pan must never boil. Bring the water to simmering point. Turn off the heat and put the chocolate pan on top. If the water gets too cool, take the chocolate container off the water pan before reheating the water. Stir the chocolate very gently, and only occasionally, as air bubbles will spoil the finished chocolates. The temperature of the chocolate should be about 45°C (110°F); if it reaches 50°C (120°F) or above it will be burnt. Chocolate should be stored at temperatures between 18°C and 20°C (65°F and 68°F) and will store (depending on the filling) for six months if the humidity is not high. The refrigerator is not a good place to store chocolate, as the chocolate develops a 'bloom' when subsequently placed at room temperature.

Coffee grinder An electric coffee grinder is invaluable for grinding seeds, dried herbs, and dried citrus skin to reduce these to a powder. If you do not have a grinder you can achieve the same results with a pestle and mortar, but in comparison it will take a very long time.

Degorge Refers to a process which rids vegetables of strong flavours and excess moisture. Eggplant is usually degorged as it contains a bitter juice which can spoil the flavour of the finished dish. Slice or cube the eggplant. Sprinkle with salt and place in a single layer in a colander and leave for 30 minutes. Rinse well.

Double boiler An essential piece of kitchen equipment if you want to make good curds, custards or chocolates. A double boiler is a pan which sits closely on top of a pan containing the hot water. A well-fitting heatproof bowl placed on a pan may be used. The top pan or bowl must never touch the water. The water is kept at simmering point—never boiling—to cook the food without direct heat.

Forming logs   To form neat logs for making biscuits, savoury butters, cheeses or sweets you will need a ruler and strong greaseproof paper or non-stick baking paper. Cut a rectangle of paper about 30 × 45 cm (12″ × 18″). Spoon your mixture along the width of the paper in a rough roll about a quarter of the way down from the top. Fold the bottom of the paper over the roll. Put the ruler where the bottom paper meets the top, enclosing the roll. Hold the top of the bottom sheet and pull the ruler steadily downwards, taking the roll with it. When the roll is to your satisfaction, fold fresh paper around it and refrigerate until firm enough to slice or otherwise deal with.

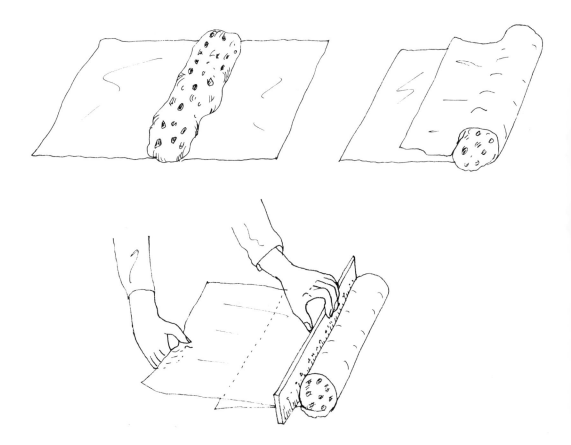

Ghee   Butter which has had the solids removed leaving pure butter fat. Ghee can be cooked at much higher temperatures than butter, without burning. It is readily available in many supermarkets and specialty shops but if you would like to make your own, heat unsalted butter gently until it froths. Spoon the froth from the top and gently pour the clear fat into a small bowl, leaving the remaining solids in the pan. Chill until firm. Scrape any residue from the bottom. Reheat and strain through muslin or cheesecloth. The ghee will keep for three or four months and need not be refrigerated unless the weather is very hot.

Horseradish   The juice of horseradish is vicious! If you have problems peeling onions then beware of horseradish as it is much stronger. I have mentioned in my book *Herbcraft* (Hodder & Stoughton, 1990) how I was once caught wearing a diving mask and snorkel while preparing horseradish—well, bizarre as it sounds, it works.

Jam and jelly making Jams need to boil very hard, so pans need to be very large to prevent boiling over and splashing. Do not stir the jam once it has come to a boil or it will crystallise.

To test for setting Do not let the jam boil for too long before testing as it can lose its setting properties if overcooked. The simplest way of testing is to take the jam off the heat and put a teaspoon of jam on a cold plate. Allow the jam on the plate to cool completely, then push the surface gently with your finger. If it wrinkles when pushed, the jam is ready, if not, put the pan back on the heat to boil a little longer.

Scum on jam Put a knob of butter in the pan while the jam is cooking and very little scum will form. The small amount rising to the top may be dispersed if the jam is stirred just before potting.

Sterilising jars Jams and jellies will keep much longer if the jars are sterilised before use. Wash well in warm soapy water, rinse and put upside-down in an oven which is set to its lowest heat. Leave for 10 minutes. Fill the jars while still hot.

Jelly bags These can be made by stitching double thicknesses of cheesecloth or muslin into rectangular bag shapes. French seams (or reinforced double seams) are necessary for strength. Make several different sizes. You will find many uses for these bags, from straining cheeses to dripping jellies.

Nuts It is sometimes possible to bulk-buy nuts inexpensively. Keep them in the freezer and they will remain fresh indefinitely.

To roast nuts Preheat the oven to 180°C (350°F). Spread the nuts in a single layer on shallow baking trays. Roast for 12–15 minutes or until the nuts are beginning to colour. Stir often. The nuts may be grilled, which is faster, but there is far more chance of burning and the cooking is not as even.

To remove the skins from hazelnuts Roast in the usual way. Cool. Rub the nuts between your hands, letting the skins fall back into the tray.

To blanch almonds Pour boiling water over the shelled almonds. Leave for a few minutes. Take the nuts out one at a time and slip the skins off between your fingers.

To 'de-bitter' walnuts The outer skin of shelled walnuts can become bitter if the nuts are not fresh. To revive them you can pour boiling water over the nuts in a basin, leave for 10 minutes and drain. Pat in a clean tea-towel to dry.

Sealing jars and bottles Air is one of the main reasons for spoilage of food. Badly fitting lids or corks allow air to enter the bottles and jars. Fill jars and bottles to within 1 cm (½") of the top. Seal with very well-fitting lids, or drip melted wax into the seam between the cork and the bottle.

Straining The initial straining of coarse vegetable matter from wines and vinegars may be done through sieves and cheesecloth bags, but the finer straining is best done through coffee filter paper. Yoghurt cheese and other cottage cheeses drain well through filter paper and none of the precious solids are lost.

Sugar boiling Sugar thermometers are the best for determining the heat of fudge and toffee mixtures. If you do not own one, you can use the following simple test by using a ½ a cup of cold water:

Soft ball Drop some mixture in the water. It should form a soft ball when rolled between the fingers.

Hard ball The mixture should hold its shape when dropped in the cold water.

Soft crack The mixture forms hard but not brittle threads in the water.

Hard crack The syrup forms hard, brittle threads in the water.

Tomatoes To peel, pour boiling water over the tomatoes to cover. Leave for a few minutes. The skin will then peel off very easily.

Weights and Measures

All spoon and cup measures in this book are standard. A cup measure set usually consists of 1 cup, ½ cup, ⅓ cup and ¼ cup. Spoon sets usually contain 1 tablespoon, ½ tablespoon, ⅓ tablespoon and ¼ tablespoon. These sets are readily available in supermarkets and kitchen stores.

Cup sizes

Cup	mL
¼	60
⅓	80
½	125
1	250

Spoon sizes

Spoon	mL
¼ teaspoon	1.25
½ teaspoon	2.5
1 teaspoon	5
1 tablespoon	20

Oven temperatures (approximate conversions)

	Fahrenheit	Celsius
very slow	250	120
slow	275–300	140–150
moderately slow	325–350	160–180
moderate	350	180
moderately hot	375	190
hot	400–450	200–230
very hot	475–500	250–260

Length

Inches	Metric
¹⁄₁₆	2 mm
¼	6 mm
⅜	1 cm
1	2.5 cm
2	5 cm
6	15 cm
12	30 cm
36	91 cm

Glossary

Allspice Sometimes called 'pimento'. Not to be confused with mixed spice. This spice from the West Indies has a combination of the flavours of nutmeg, mace, and cloves. It can be used in both sweet and savoury cooking.

Chillies or peppers Small, hot peppers. As a rule the smaller the chilli, the hotter and more pungent the flavour. The hottest parts of the chilli are the seeds, which are usually discarded. Chillies contain an oil called 'capsaicin' which can cause blistering and burning, so great care needs to be taken during preparation (see p.9).

Chilli powder The hottest ground chilli is Asian. The Mexican variety is often mixed with cumin and other spices to give a milder flavour.

Cornflour A refined flour ground from corn. Used to thicken sauces and for giving a very 'short' quality to biscuits. Arrowroot may be substituted.

Ghee Otherwise known as 'clarified butter'. Ghee is butter which has been clarified to remove milk solids, making a product which does not burn as readily as butter when used for frying. Ghee is readily available in supermarkets and specialty stores but if you would like to make your own, the method will be found on p.10.

Oil, olive The best oil to use for many types of cooking, particularly Italian. The low 'smoking point' makes it unsuitable for deep-frying. The best olive oil to use is 'virgin'; this is the first oil crushed from the olives, is quite green and full of flavour. The yellower oils have usually been heated, which destroys some flavour and some natural properties of the oil.

Oil, safflower An excellent oil for all cooking where the flavour of olive oil is unsuitable or too strong. It is high in polyunsaturated fats and has very little flavour of its own.

Pickling spice A mixture of spices used to flavour pickles and marinated vegetables (see p.58).

Rosewater Distilled water with the essential oil of roses added. A stronger version called either 'rose essence' or 'rose concentrate' may also be found. Add in drops only until the desired flavour is achieved. Rosewater is stocked by most pharmacies.

Shallots or eschalots In Australia the name 'shallot' is given incorrectly to the spring onion. The true shallot is small, with a purple tinge and has reddish-brown skin. It grows in bulb form and is divided into sections, similar to garlic. It is milder than onions and is delicious in any cooking where a mild onion flavour is needed.

Soda bicarbonate Also known as 'baking soda' or 'bicarbonate of soda'. It is a raising agent used in some cakes and biscuits. Half a teaspoon mixed with 1 teaspoon of cream of tartar is equal to 2 teaspoons baking powder.

Spring onions or scallions Members of the onion family. They are mild-flavoured with a small white bulb and long slender green leaves. Used mainly in salads, sandwiches, and garnishes.

Vinegar, cider Made from fermented apples and smells strongly of cider. Use where the distinctive flavour adds to the other flavours without overpowering them.

Vinegar, coconut   Fermented and distilled sap of the coconut palm. This is a lovely vinegar to use in Asian cookery. It is quite mild so if another vinegar is substituted it should be diluted.

Vinegar, malt   Brewed from barley, this vinegar has a strong, mildly bitter flavour and is best used in pickles and sauces.

Vinegar, rice and palm   These delicate vinegars are available from Asian food stores.

Vinegar, spiced   Malt vinegar is the best to use for spicing. The vinegar is mainly used for making pickles and sauces. A recipe will be found on p.58.

Vinegar, wine   Expensive but delicious vinegars are made from fermented wines. Because of the cost involved it's better to use these vinegars where their flavour will be most appreciated (as in dressings, marinades, and delicate sauces).

Zest   The outer, thin skin of the citrus fruit, which contains the essential oils. It can be removed with tools called 'zesters' or may be grated—care being taken not to remove any of the white pith.

Savoury Gifts

The gentle art of gastronomy is a friendly one. It hurdles the language barrier,
makes friends among civilized people and warms the heart . . .

—Samuel Chamberlain (1895–1975)

You will notice that in many of the recipes I give the option of using either olive or safflower oil. The reason for this is that while olive oil has a wonderful flavour, it solidifies if refrigerated and you have to remember to remove the jar or dish from the refrigerator at least 30 minutes before you need it. If you don't want to have to do this you can substitute safflower oil, which stays liquid even when very cold.

Non-metallic caps and lids must be used for any recipe containing vinegar to prevent the poisonous interaction between acid and metal.

It is most important that as little room as possible is left between the top of the jar and the contents. Air is a major spoiler of food. Caps should fit well to prevent air entering the container.

Glass jars and bottles need to be kept in the dark if possible—light is destructive to food and also spoils the appearance by bleaching out a lot of colour.

Fresh herbs are used throughout unless dried are specified. If you do not have access to fresh herbs, then dried herbs may be substituted and the amount of herb reduced by two-thirds.

MARINADES & NUTS

PICKLED MUSHROOMS

These will keep for several weeks if sealed in an airtight container. Once opened they should be kept in the refrigerator.

button mushrooms	*500 g (1 lb)*	Simmer for 10 minutes. Drain,
white wine vinegar	*1 cup*	reserve liquid.
water	*1 cup*	
salt	*1 teaspoon*	
black pepper	*½ teaspoon*	
small, fresh red chillies	*5*	Layer all with the mushrooms in a
bay leaves	*3*	wide-mouthed jar. Pour reserved
lemon thyme sprigs	*4*	liquid over to within 5 cm (2")
garlic cloves, sliced	*3*	from the top. Cover with 2.5 cm
coriander seeds	*12*	(1") olive oil. Seal and store in a
cloves, whole	*6*	cool place.
peppercorns	*12*	
rosemary	*2 sprigs 5 cm (2") long*	

OPPOSITE
Gifts can be packaged in boxes, bottles, paper, jars and baskets (see pp.121–134).

DILL PICKLES

cider vinegar	*4 cups*	Bring to the boil. Allow to cool.
water	*2 cups*	
salt	*½ cup*	
gherkins or small cucumbers		Layer all in a jar or crock with a
garlic	*3 cloves*	wide mouth. Pour brine over.
bay leaves	*3 leaves*	Cover. Leave one week before
dill seeds	*3 tablespoons*	using. The jar can have more
mixed pickling spice	*1 tablespoon*	gherkins added as they are used.

PICKLED NASTURTIUM SEEDS

These can take the place of capers; I find them much tastier and better textured.

Soak the seeds in a brine made from 1 heaped tablespoon of salt dissolved in 1½ cups of water—this should just cover the seeds. Increase or decrease these quantities depending on the number of seeds you have. Change the brine every day for 3 days. Rinse seeds well, put in a jar and cover with either white wine or cider vinegar. Leave 5-6 weeks before using.

BRANDIED TOMATOES

These tomatoes add colour and zest to a salad and are good to eat with cheese and bread or crackers. They will store for quite a few weeks in the refrigerator if they are well covered with the liquid and sealed tightly.

cherry tomatoes	*300 g (9 oz)*	Pierce a hole through the centre of each with a skewer.
brandy	*¼–½ cup*	Shake together in a jar until well
olive or safflower oil	*½ cup*	blended. Mix carefully with the
lemon juice	*2 teaspoons*	tomatoes. Spoon into a jar,
basil, chopped	*1 tablespoon*	making sure that the tomatoes are
sugar, white	*2 teaspoons*	well covered. Seal.
lemon zest (see p.14)	*1 teaspoon*	
spring onion, chopped	*1*	
cinnamon stick	*2.5 cm (1")*	
salt and black pepper	*to taste*	

OPPOSITE
A breakfast basket might include golden granola, citrus pikelets, marmalade, tea mix, sherried apricots and peaches, and a selection of sweet butters (see also p.131).

PICKLED EGGPLANT

The texture of this eggplant is chewy and satisfying. It keeps very well in the refrigerator. Serve as a side dish with cheese and bread or as part of an antipasto platter.

eggplant cooking salt	*1 large* *¼–½ cup*	Slice into strips approximately index-finger size. Mix well with the salt, put into a colander and leave for 6 hours. Squeeze until you can get no more liquid out—it is important to do this well. Rinse lightly. Put in a bowl.
malt vinegar water		Pour over in equal quantities to cover. Leave for 2 hours. Squeeze very well, as before.
fresh oregano fresh basil garlic cloves, sliced red chilli, sliced	*2 sprigs* *4 sprigs* *2* *1*	Layer with the eggplant in small jars.
olive or safflower oil	*to cover*	Pour over to cover. Leave for one week before using.

MIDDLE EASTERN EGGPLANTS

Another totally delicious traditional eggplant recipe which can be made with the small end-of-season eggplants (no longer than 10 cm [4"] long). They should be stored in the refrigerator and will then keep for three to four months if tightly sealed.

baby eggplants, stems removed salt	*2 kg (4 lb)* *2 teaspoons*	Boil in a large pan until cooked but still firm, about 7 minutes. Drain, cool and cut a deep lengthwise pocket in each. Put in a colander, slit side down and leave to drain for 12 hours.
garlic, crushed walnuts, finely crushed olive oil	*2 tablespoons* *1½ cups* *2 teaspoons*	Mix together, divide evenly between the eggplants, stuffing the pockets. Press each eggplant closed, replace in the colander slit side down and leave to drain for a further 6 hours. Pack carefully into large, wide-mouthed jars.
white wine vinegar olive oil		⅔ fill the jars with vinegar, top up with water, leaving space for 2.5 cm (1") of olive oil on top. Seal well.

MARINATED CAPSICUM SALAD

These capsicums are tasty as a side-dish or to eat with cheese. Leave for a few days before eating. They can be stored in the refrigerator for about one month.

red capsicums	*4*	Cut the capsicums into chunks.
green capsicums	*4*	Put into a pan of boiling water. Cook for 3 minutes. Drain well. Cool.
red wine vinegar	*6 tablespoons*	Mix all well together. Layer with
medium dry sherry	*2 tablespoons*	the capsicums in a wide-mouthed
Worcestershire sauce	*1 tablespoon*	jar making sure that the
olive or safflower oil	*6 tablespoons*	vegetables are well covered.
salt	*1 teaspoon*	
black pepper	*½ teaspoon*	
sugar	*2 teaspoons*	
paprika	*1 teaspoon*	
black olives, stoned & chopped	*16*	

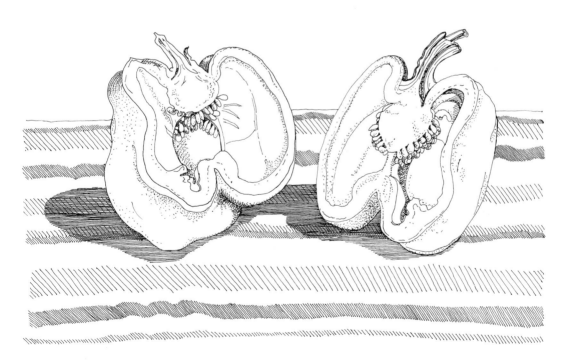

MEDITERRANEAN RED CAPSICUMS

There is always a dish of these capsicums in my refrigerator. The smoky, earthy flavour gives a lift to many otherwise boring foods. Use them in salads, as a side-dish or in sandwiches and on pizzas. Your friends will want the recipe, so maybe you could attach a recipe card to the jar. The capsicums will keep in the refrigerator for up to three weeks (they will vanish long before this).

Preheat oven to 200°C (400°F).

red capsicums	6	Put directly on a shelf in the oven. Roast until very soft and beginning to scorch. Put in a plastic bag, fold the top over and leave to go cold. Remove the skin and seeds. Slice into strips.
rosemary	4 sprigs	Layer with the capsicums in a wide-mouthed jar.
garlic, sliced	1 clove	
black peppercorns	1 teaspoon	
cider vinegar	2 tablespoons	
olive or safflower oil	to cover	Top up with oil to cover completely. Seal the jar.

PICKLED EGGS

Good to have on hand for snacks, sandwiches, salads and other dishes. Leave for three to four days before using. If refrigerated, the eggs will keep for several weeks.

eggs, shelled and hard boiled	12	
lemon thyme, fresh	2 sprigs	Layer with the eggs in a wide-mouthed jar.
oregano, fresh	2 sprigs	
rosemary, fresh	1 sprig	
peppercorns, green and black	2 tablespoons	
garlic cloves, sliced	2	
spiced vinegar (see p.58)	about 4 cups	Heat to below boiling point and pour over the eggs.

ESCABECHE

This is a Mexican recipe which will keep for at least two weeks if stored in a covered container in the refrigerator. There is also a recipe for Escabeche dressing (see p.64).

plain flour	*1 cup*	The fillets should not be too thick, so slice if needed. Flour the fish, shake off the surplus.
fish fillets, white, firm	*1 kg (2 lb)*	
olive or safflower oil	*2 tablespoons*	Melt together in a frypan. Brown the fish for 3–4 minutes on both sides. Drain well. Transfer to a shallow dish.
butter	*2 tablespoons*	
oranges, rind only from	*2*	Cut into the thinnest possible slices. Don't use any white pith.
red capsicums	*1*	Cut the capsicums into delicate strips. Arrange with rind over the fish.
green capsicums	*1*	
garlic, crushed	*2 cloves*	Combine all these ingredients. Pour over the fish. Cover. Leave for a day before using.
coriander, fresh	*1 tablespoon*	
salt	*½ teaspoon*	
black pepper, coarse	*½ teaspoon*	
brown sugar	*1 tablespoon*	
capers	*¼ cup*	
bay leaves	*2*	
orange juice	*¼ cup*	
white wine	*⅓ cup*	
white wine vinegar	*⅓ cup*	

MARINATED FETTA

Leave for about a week before using, to allow the full flavour to develop. The cheese will keep for several weeks. I like to use low-salt fetta both for flavour and health reasons. Other cheeses may be preserved in this manner; other types of goats' cheese are particularly nice. Store in the refrigerator.

fetta	*1 kg (2 lb)*	Cut into 2.5 cm (1″) cubes.
black mustard seed	*1 tablespoon*	Layer with the cheese in a jar with a well-fitting lid.
white mustard seed	*1 tablespoon*	
black pepper seed	*2 tablespoons*	
bay leaves	*2*	
red chillies	*2 whole*	
olive or safflower oil		Pour into the jar covering the contents completely. Seal.

ROLLMOPS

Even amateur fisherpersons seem to be able to catch herrings. Here is a delicious way to preserve surplus herrings. The rollmops will keep for one month under refrigeration.

herrings	6	Fillet but leave the skins on.
pickled gherkins	6	Cut each gherkin in half lengthwise and roll the fillets, skin-side out, around the gherkin. Fasten with toothpicks.
lemon, sliced	1	Layer with the herrings in a wide-mouthed jar leaving some lemon slices for the last layer.
onion, medium, sliced	2	
bay leaves	4	
mustard seed	½ teaspoon	
fennel seed	½ teaspoon	
chilli peppers, dried	2	
malt vinegar	2 cups	Bring all to boiling point. Cool. Pour over the contents of the jar. Seal the jar and keep in the refrigerator for a week before using.
cloves	4	
water	¼ cup	
salt	2 teaspoons	

JERKY

This is fun to make and would be very suitable for someone who 'backpacks'. If the drying has been done well, and the jerky is stored in an airtight container, it will keep for months.

Preheat the oven to 150°C (300°F) or lower.

lean round beef	1 kg (2 lb)	Freeze until very firm. Cut into slices 0.5 cm (¼") wide and then into strips 4 cm (1½") long.
soya sauce	¼ cup	Mix all these ingredients well. Put the meat strips in a shallow dish and pour the marinade over. Cover the dish and refrigerate for 24 hours, stirring often. Drain the meat well and pat dry. Put the oven racks on the lowest shelf, leaving the oven door slightly open. Spread the meat on the racks, keeping the pieces separate. The jerky is ready when the meat is brown and dry.
Worcestershire sauce	1 tablespoon	
black pepper, ground	¼ teaspoon	
garlic powder	¼ teaspoon	
onion powder	¼ teaspoon	
paprika	¼ teaspoon	

Olives

Olives in flavoured oil look as good as they taste. Any good olives may be used; my favourites are Kalamato olives—rich, fruity and Greek. The best oil to use is olive, but if the olives are to be stored in the refrigerator it's probably better to use safflower, as olive oil goes solid when very cold. Olives need to be stored in a cool place and if kept in the refrigerator will keep for months. The oil may be used for cooking or in dressings when the olives have been eaten.

CITRUS OLIVES

olives	500 g (1 lb)	Rinse and drain.
peel of one lemon, no pith peel of one orange, no pith		Cut into strips about 1 cm (½″) wide by 5 cm (2″) long.
black peppercorns cardamom seeds	2 teaspoons 2 teaspoons	Bruise the seeds but don't crush them, then layer with the olives in a wide-mouthed jar. Cover with oil. Leave for one week before using.

THYME AND GARLIC OLIVES

olives	500 g (1 lb)	Rinse and drain.
thyme, fresh garlic cloves, peeled cumin seed black peppercorns	2 × 10 cm (4″) 5 1 teaspoon 1 teaspoon	Cut the garlic cloves in half. Layer all with the olives in a wide-mouthed jar. Cover with oil. Leave for one week before using.

LEMON OLIVES

olives	500 g (1 lb)	Rinse and drain.
lemon slices, thick fennel leaves, chopped coriander seeds garlic cloves, sliced	8 handful 1 tablespoon 3	Layer with the olives in a wide-mouthed jar. Cover with oil. Leave for one week before using.

MARINATED OLIVES

olives	500 g (1 lb)	Rinse and drain.
red capsicum, thinly sliced	½	Combine all these ingredients in a
green capsicum, thinly sliced	½	wide-mouthed jar. Cover with oil.
garlic cloves, sliced	2	Leave for one week before using.
lemon thyme	2 sprigs	
bay leaves	2	
oregano	2 sprigs	
lemon peel	3 strips	

Nuts

Flavoured nuts are delicious at any time of the day. They can be taken on picnics and walks, children enjoy them as a snack and also in their lunch boxes—the list is long and the biggest problem would be having enough of these delectable morsels at all times. You will find hints on roasting, blanching, and storing nuts on p.11.

CURRIED ALMONDS

Preheat oven to 180°C (350°F).

almonds, blanched	2 cups	Mix in a shallow baking tin. Roast
garlic oil (see p.60)	1 tablespoon	until golden brown. Drain on
		paper towel.
curry powder	2 teaspoons	Mix together. Add nuts. Return to
salt	1 teaspoon	pan. Cook for a further 4-6
garlic powder	½ teaspoon	minutes, stirring often. Cool. Store
		in an airtight container.

DEVILLED ALMONDS

Preheat oven to 180°C (350°F).

almonds, unblanched garlic oil (see p.60)	2 cups 1 tablespoon	Mix. Roast until just beginning to brown. Drain on paper towel.
Worcestershire sauce soya sauce salt black pepper chilli powder	1 teaspoon 1 teaspoon ½ teaspoon pinch pinch	Mix together. Add nuts. Return to the oven for about 4 minutes, stirring often. Cool and store in an airtight container.

MIXED DEVILLED NUTS

garlic, crushed olive oil	2 cloves 2 tablespoons	Sauté together for 2 minutes, stirring.
mixed nuts	2 cups	Add. Fry till golden. Remove and drain on paper towel.
paprika chilli powder salt pepper onion powder	1 teaspoon ⅛ teaspoon ½ teaspoon ⅛ teaspoon ½ teaspoon	Mix together in a bowl. Add the hot nuts. Toss well. Cool. Store in an airtight container.

MEXICAN PEANUTS

olive oil	1 tablespoon	Heat in a frypan.
blanched raw peanuts	2 cups	Add. Sauté till light brown. Stir continuously.
chilli powder garlic, crushed	⅛ teaspoon 1 small clove	Add. Sauté together for a few minutes.
cumin powder coriander powder	⅛ teaspoon ¼ teaspoon	Add. Sauté one minute more.
salt	½ teaspoon	Add. Remove from heat. Stir well. Allow to cool. Store in an airtight container.

SOYA SUNNIES

sunflower seeds	*2 cups*	Toast in a small saucepan until golden brown. Stir constantly.
soya sauce, low-salt	*2 tablespoons*	Add to the seeds in the hot pan. Stir over a low heat until the sauce has completely evaporated. Spread in a single layer to cool. Store in an airtight jar.

SPICY PEPS

Use pepitas (hulled Mexican pumpkin seeds) if you can get them. If not, any hulled pumpkin seeds will be acceptable.

pepitas	*2 cups*	Roast in a small pan until golden brown. Stir continuously. Proceed as for curried almonds (see p.24).
olive oil	*1 tablespoon*	

PÂTÉS & CHEESES

We may live without friends, we may live without books,
But civilized man cannot live without cooks.
                    —E.W. Bulwer-Lytton (1831–91)

Pâtés

Pâtés can be served with pickled or fresh vegetables and crusty bread for a healthy and appetising lunch, used as a spread in sandwiches, or served with crackers for a pre-dinner or entrée course. If the pots are well packed to exclude air, topped with ghee (p.10) and stored in a refrigerator, most pâtés will keep up to two weeks. Decorate with herbs, orange slices or any other suitable garnish immediately before giving as a gift.

CHICKEN LIVER PÂTÉ WITH COINTREAU

This is a pâté with an Italian influence. We once owned a restaurant called 'The Prancing Pony' and served this pâté with monotonous regularity. Whenever we tried to take it off the menu the regular customers would become very upset.

chicken livers	*500 g (1 lb)*	Wash well. Trim any skin or fat, and chop.
butter onion, diced	*¼ cup* *1 cup*	Sauté together until onion is soft. Add livers and cook until the livers change colour. Don't overcook.
black olives, stoned paprika fresh lemon thyme, chopped salt black pepper Cointreau or brandy	*4* *½ teaspoon* *½ teaspoon* *½ teaspoon* *½ teaspoon* *1 tablespoon*	Blend with liver mixture until smooth. Pack in dishes. See opening remarks on pâtés (above) to proceed.

SMOKED HERRING PÂTÉ

smoked herrings	*1 tin*	Blend till smooth.
butter eggs, beaten salt and pepper chilli powder	*½ cup* *2* *to taste* *pinch*	Cook in a double boiler (see p.9) until the egg thickens. Take care not to overcook. Scrape into a blender with the herrings.
cream cheese thick mayonnaise	*½ cup* *¼ cup*	Add, blend all until smooth, scrape into a bowl, stir occasionally until cool. Pot. See opening remarks on pâtés (above) to proceed.

SMOKED OYSTER PÂTÉ

gelatine powder	*1 teaspoon*	Sprinkle over the hot water, stir till dissolved. This step is optional. If you like a soft dip-type pâté it may be omitted.
hot water	*1 tablespoon*	
ricotta	*¼ cup*	Mix with gelatine. Blend all till very smooth. Check seasoning.
butter, softened	*¼ cup*	
yoghurt, thick	*¼ cup*	
capers	*2 tablespoons*	
salt & black pepper	*to taste*	
mixed dried herbs	*¼ teaspoon*	
thick mayonnaise	*2 tablespoons*	
fresh parsley, chopped	*1 tablespoon*	
tins of smoked oysters, drained	*2 × 105 g (3½ oz)*	Chop very finely. Add to above, mix well. The oysters may be blended with the above but some people find the colour off-putting! See opening remarks on pâtés (p.28) to proceed.

LIVER AND BRANDY PÂTÉ

butter, softened	*½ cup*	Sauté all until the onion and bacon are cooked.
onion, finely chopped	*½*	
garlic, crushed	*2 cloves*	
bacon, finely chopped	*2 rashers*	
chicken livers, trimmed	*250 g*	Add, cook for 5 minutes. Take off the heat. Put in a blender.
thyme, fresh	*¼ teaspoon*	Add to blender, process until smooth. See opening remarks on pâtés (p.28) to proceed.
oregano, fresh	*¼ teaspoon*	
cracked black pepper	*shake*	
salt	*to taste*	
sour cream	*2 tablespoons*	
brandy	*1 tablespoon*	

The following recipes are for vegetarian pâtés. They are full of flavour and are sure to please your non meat-eating friends. They should be potted and topped with ghee (see p.10) in the same way as other pâtés.

RICOTTA AND WALNUT PÂTÉ

ricotta	½ cup	Blend all well together. Wrap in a clean cloth and leave in the refrigerator until some of the moisture is absorbed. Pack into a dish or ramekins. See opening remarks on pâtés (p.28) to proceed.
cream cheese	½ cup	
parmesan, grated	2 tablespoons	
walnuts, chopped	½ cup	
garlic, finely crushed	1 clove	
lemon juice	1 tablespoon	
parsley, finely chopped	¼ cup	
safflower oil	2 tablespoons	
salt & black pepper	to taste	

MUSHROOM PÂTÉ

butter	125 g (¼ lb)	Cook together until onion is soft but not brown.
onion, chopped	1	
garlic, crushed	2 cloves	
celery, minced	2 sticks	
mushrooms, finely chopped	250 g (½ lb)	Add, cook 5 minutes.
cream cheese	1 cup	Add all, blend till smooth.
lemon zest (see p.14)	1 level teaspoon	
mushroom ketchup	2 teaspoons	
salt	½ teaspoon	
black pepper	to taste	
double cream	¼ cup	Add, mix well. See opening remarks on pâtés (p.28) to proceed.

Potted Cheeses

Use your favourite cheddar in these recipes. Most recipes call for strong cheddar but some people (myself included) find the flavour overpowering when mixed with other ingredients. For storage, treat potted cheese in the same way as pâtés by topping with a layer of ghee (see p.10). These cheeses can be used as a dip with vegetable sticks, as sandwich fillings or as a savoury on toast. They will keep for about three to four weeks if refrigerated and well covered.

WALNUT CHEESE POT

cheddar cheese, grated	2½ cups	Mix all together until smooth. If the consistency is too dry a little more melted butter may be mixed in. Pack into small pots or ramekins. See above for general comments on potted cheeses.
butter, softened	2 tablespoons	
Worcestershire sauce	1 teaspoon	
medium dry sherry	3 tablespoons	
walnuts, finely chopped	½ cup	
black pepper, cracked	1 teaspoon	
nutmeg	pinch	

CHEESE CROCK

cheddar	3 cups	Blend all well together. Pot. Leave a few days before using. See p.30 for general comments on potted cheeses.
cream cheese	½ cup	
olive oil	1 tablespoon	
made mustard	½ teaspoon	
onion powder	1 teaspoon	
paprika	½ teaspoon	
sherry, medium dry	1 tablespoon	
celery salt	½ teaspoon	

CHEESE BALL

An interesting and colourful lunch table centrepiece which tastes as good as it looks. The quantities can be adapted to make whatever size of ball needed. If the ball is being given as a gift it's better to leave the final nut or herb coating until just before needed, as this will give a fresher appearance. This cheese ball may 'collapse' a little if the weather is very warm, so keep refrigerated until the last minute. The ball may be studded with toasted pine nuts instead of chives if desired. The appearance of the ball is beautiful if you use chopped, flat leaved garlic chives as well as the common chives.

cream cheese	125 g (¼ lb)	Blend all very well together. Spoon into plastic wrap, shape into a ball and refrigerate for at least one hour. Unwrap and roll in chopped chives. Re-wrap in plastic which has had a few holes pierced in it, and store in the refrigerator.
mild cheddar, finely grated	60 g (2 oz)	
salt	¼ teaspoon	
fresh chives, finely chopped	1 tablespoon	
fresh parsley, finely chopped	1 tablespoon	
spring onions, finely chopped	1 tablespoon	
black pepper, cracked	sprinkle	
Worcestershire sauce	½ teaspoon	

GOURMET POTTED CHEESE

Camembert, softened	125 g (¼ lb)	Chop and put in a blender.
cream cheese	250 g (½ lb)	Add. Blend all well together. Pot.
ricotta	1 cup	Leave for 24 hours to mature
parmesan, grated	½ cup	before using. A little sherry may
dried mixed herbs	½ teaspoon	be added if a softer consistency is
salt & black pepper	to taste	desired. See above for general
		comments on potted cheeses.

SPICY CHEESE CROCK

cheddar, grated	2 cups	Mix all thoroughly.
ricotta	½ cup	
garlic, crushed finely	1 clove	
Worcestershire sauce	1 teaspoon	
grainy mustard	1 teaspoon	
dried mixed herbs	1 teaspoon	
chilli powder	pinch	
salt & cracked pepper	to taste	
butter, softened	2 tablespoons	
beer, flat	¼–½ cup	Add enough to give a good consistency. Pot. Mature 3 days before use.

YOGHURT CHEESE BALLS

This is a version of a Middle Eastern dish called 'Labneh'. To make it you need either thick homemade yoghurt or a Greek-type yoghurt. The average supermarket product which passes for yoghurt won't do as it hasn't enough body.

Line a funnel with a large coffee filter bag, stand in a jug, spoon the yoghurt into the bag and leave to drip in the refrigerator for at least 12 hours. It should then be firm enough to form into balls. Don't leave it for too long or it will become over-sour.

Roll the yoghurt cheese into walnut-sized balls and roll in paprika. Layer in wide-necked jars with sprigs of thyme and oregano, and a bay leaf. Sprinkle a few peppercorns and a few slivers of garlic cloves among the balls. Cover completely with olive or safflower oil and leave in the refrigerator for a week to mature before use. The balls will need to be kept refrigerated and will keep for several weeks or even months.

Herbed Olives

Chinese Mixed Vegetables

Passionfruit Squash

Cointreau Oranges

Zucchini Pickle

Mexican Mustard

HERB CHEESE POT

grated cheddar	1 cup	Using a chopper blade, blend
chives, chopped	3 teaspoons	until very fine.
thyme, chopped	½ teaspoon	
oregano, chopped	½ teaspoon	
cream cheese	½ cup	Add, blend till smooth. Pack in
yoghurt	¼ cup	lidded pots pouring a little oil or
black pepper, coarsely ground	¼ teaspoon	ghee over. See p.30 for general
salt	¼ teaspoon	comments on potted cheeses.
medium dry sherry	1 tablespoon	

FARMHOUSE POTTED CHEESE

grated cheddar	1 cup	Blend well.
ricotta or neufchâtel	½ cup	
sweet pickle	¼ cup	Add, blend until well mixed. Pot.
sherry, medium dry	1 tablespoon	See p.30 for general comments on
mayonnaise	1 tablespoon	potted cheeses.
French mustard	1 teaspoon	
black pepper, coarsely ground	pinch	

PREVIOUS PAGE
A lunch basket might include passionfruit cordial, cracked-pepper crackers, liver and brandy pâté, Mexican mustard, oranges in Cointreau, thyme and garlic olives, mixed devilled nuts, and a selection of pickles (see also p.131).

OPPOSITE
A tea-time basket might include cheese straws, apricot rings, kippferl, almond shortbread, macaroons, chocolate chip brownies, chocolate dipped butter-biscuits, Chinese lemon tea, and spicy gingerbread (see also p.131).

BUTTERS & SAUCES

The discovery of a new dish does more for the happiness of man than the discovery of a star.

—Brillat-Savarin

Flavoured Butters

Flavoured butters are easy to make and have many uses. They can enliven an otherwise boring sandwich, can be smeared on steaks or fish, can be dabbed on vegetables or swirled through pasta. Closely covered they will keep for three weeks to one month in the refrigerator or may be kept frozen for three months. The butters may be formed into logs (see p.10), packed into jars or into small ramekins. A set of six ramekins each containing a different butter makes a lovely gift.

LEMON AND MUSTARD BUTTER

butter, softened	*1 cup*	Mix all well together. See above
grainy mustard	*2 tablespoons*	for packaging and storing hints.
lemon juice	*2 teaspoons*	
black pepper	*pinch*	

HERB BUTTER 1

butter, softened	*1 cup*	Blend all well together. See above
parsley, chopped finely	*2 tablespoons*	for packaging and storing hints.
chives, chopped finely	*2 tablespoons*	
mint, chopped finely	*1 tablespoon*	
mustard powder	*1 teaspoon*	
pepper	*good pinch*	

HERB BUTTER 2

butter, softened	*1 cup*	Beat all well together.
basil, chopped	*2 tablespoons*	
French sorrel, chopped	*2 tablespoons*	
lemon juice	*2 tablespoons*	Add drop by drop, beating well until blended. See above for packaging and storing hints.

DEVILLED BUTTER

butter, softened	*1 cup*	Cream all well together. See
grainy mustard	*2 tablespoons*	above for packaging and storing
Worcestershire sauce	*4 tablespoons*	hints.
garlic, crushed finely	*2 cloves*	
onion, grated	*2 tablespoons*	
chilli powder	*good pinch*	

GARLIC BUTTER

I rarely find enough garlic to suit my taste so you might find this recipe overpowering! Two tablespoons of herbs and a spring onion may be added to make a change.

butter, softened	*1 cup*	Blend well together.
garlic, finely crushed	*4 cloves*	

ANCHOVY BUTTER

butter, softened	1 cup	Cream together until the lemon
canned anchovies, pureed	90 g (3 oz)	juice is completely blended. See
chilli powder	¼ teaspoon	above for packaging and storing
lemon juice	2 teaspoons	hints.
parsley, finely chopped	1 tablespoon	

Sweet Butters

These butters are delicious spread on toast, muffins, tea breads, and plain cakes. A log (see p.10) of one of these butters, wrapped in foil and fastened like a Christmas cracker, could be given in a tea basket with instructions to cut the butter into round pats before serving. Refrigerate the butter until just before giving away.

SPICE BUTTER

butter, softened	1 cup	Mix all very well. See above for
mixed ground spice *or* cinnamon		packaging and storing hints.
or nutmeg	1 tablespoon	
light brown sugar	1 teaspoon	

BRANDY BUTTER

butter, softened	1 cup	Beat together until pale.
castor sugar	½ cup	
brandy	2 tablespoons	Beat in. See above for packaging and storage hints.

ORANGE BUTTER

butter, softened	1 cup	Beat together until well blended.
orange zest (see p.14)	1 teaspoon	See above for packaging and
orange juice	1 teaspoon	storage hints.

Sauces

WORCESTERSHIRE SAUCE

malt vinegar	*2½ cups*	Boil, covered, for 15 minutes in a non-aluminium pan.
garlic, crushed	*4 cloves*	
onion, chopped	*1 large*	
chilli powder	*2 teaspoons*	Add. Boil, covered, for 30 minutes. Cool, pour into a large jar, cover and leave for 6 weeks. Shake the jar twice a week. Strain well through a double tea-towel. Bottle.
cloves, whole	*8*	
black peppercorns	*12*	
cinnamon	*5 cm (2″)*	
horseradish, grated	*2 teaspoons*	
soya sauce	*¼ cup*	
black treacle	*2 teaspoons*	
anchovy sauce	*2 teaspoons*	
malt vinegar	*2½ cups*	
ginger root, bruised	*3 pieces 2.5 cm (1″) square*	

MUSHROOM KETCHUP

A tasty, useful ketchup for flavouring soups, pies, gravies and casseroles. This sauce will keep indefinitely but probably won't get the opportunity. Use field mushrooms if you can get them otherwise buy the largest, flattest mushrooms as these have more flavour than the tiny button variety.

mushrooms	*1 kg (2 lb)*	Clean and break into pieces.
ale (not lager)	*2½ cups*	Place all with the mushrooms in a heavy, non-aluminium pan. Cover, simmer on a low light until the contents are reduced by a half. Strain through several layers of cheesecloth (see p.9). Bring to the boil again. Pour into hot sterile bottles. Store in a cool place. Shake well before using.
vinegar, malt	*5 cups*	
anchovies, washed	*90 g (3 oz)*	
spring onions	*250 g (½ lb)*	
mace, ground	*1 teaspoon*	
cloves, ground	*1 teaspoon*	
salt	*1 teaspoon*	
black pepper, ground	*1 teaspoon*	

CHILLI SAUCE

This is a fiery sauce which may be adapted to your taste by varying the amount of chillies and mustard. As well as being excellent with meat and rice it is useful for adding a few drops to soups and casseroles which might otherwise be a little bland. Please see pp.9 and 11 for hints on dealing with chillies and peeling tomatoes before embarking on this recipe.

onions, large, minced	2	Bring all to the boil in a non-aluminium saucepan. Simmer until thickened—about one hour—stirring often to prevent burning. Allow to cool a little. Blend or rub through a sieve. Pour into hot sterilised bottles. Seal with non-metal lids.
garlic cloves, crushed	3	
black pepper	1 teaspoon	
salt	1 teaspoon	
red chillies, chopped	12	
sugar	1 tablespoon	
coriander, ground	½ teaspoon	
cumin, ground	½ teaspoon	
malt vinegar	1½ cups	
mustard, dry	1 tablespoon	
tomatoes, skinned, chopped	6	
water	½ cup	

CRANBERRY RELISH

onion, finely chopped	1 large	Fry gently in a little oil for 3 minutes. Add to other ingredients.
cranberry sauce	2 × 250 ml jars	Combine all in a non-aluminium saucepan. Bring slowly to a boil. Simmer for 30 minutes, stirring often. Spoon into hot jars, seal and leave in a cool place for a week before use.
fresh oregano, chopped	½ cup	
red wine vinegar	1 cup	
fresh basil, chopped	1 cup	
lemon peel & juice	1 lemon	
sultanas, chopped	½ cup	
soft brown sugar	2 tablespoons	
cinnamon	½ teaspoon	
salt	½ teaspoon	
pepper	pinch	

FRUIT SAUCE

This is a relief after the hot sauces! A mild tasty sauce which goes well with cheese and cold meats.

onions, peeled, chopped	6	Blend or mince all to a pulp, adding a little vinegar if needed. Put into a heavy, non-aluminium saucepan.
garlic cloves, crushed	3 cloves	
cooking apples, peeled, chopped	8	
pears, peeled, chopped	4	
celery, chopped	2 cups	
sultanas	½ cup	
salt	1 tablespoon	Add all above to the pan. Bring slowly to the boil. Simmer until thickened, 1–2 hours, stirring often. Adjust seasoning. Rub through a sieve. Bottle when cold using vinegar-proof caps.
cinnamon	2 teaspoons	
allspice	1 teaspoon	
nutmeg	1 teaspoon	
black treacle	1 cup	
dark brown sugar	2 cups	
malt vinegar	2 cups	

MEXICAN SALSA

A sauce which keeps for two to three weeks if covered and stored in the refrigerator. The salsa goes well with all Mexican foods but is also great with barbecued meats and fish. The sauce may be diluted with water just before use if a thinner consistency is liked. If you can't buy fresh jalapeno peppers use the canned variety. Please check with chilli precautions (p.9) before making this recipe.

spring onions, finely chopped	1 bunch	Mix all well together. Allow to blend for at least 4 hours before use. Store in the refrigerator in a jar with a well-fitting, vinegar-proof lid.
garlic, crushed	2 cloves	
red peppers, seeded, chopped	2	
coriander, finely chopped	⅛ cup	
jalapeno pepper, finely chopped	4	
tomatoes, skinned, chopped	6	
ground cumin	1 teaspoon	
chilli powder	pinch	
pepper sauce	to taste	
cider vinegar	4 tablespoons	
salt	to taste	
black pepper	to taste	

CHEESE SAUCE

This is a tasty sauce to fold through pasta or serve over vegetables. It stores in the refrigerator for about three weeks if container is sealed tightly.

cheddar, grated	3½ cups	Melt together in a double boiler
parmesan, grated	½ cup	(see p.9)
evaporated milk	1 cup	
French mustard	1 teaspoon	Stir in and mix gently until
salt	½ teaspoon	smooth. Spoon into small jars. To
black pepper, cracked	½ teaspoon	use, reheat in a double boiler,
Worcestershire sauce	1 teaspoon	adding milk to thin.
or dried mixed herbs	1 teaspoon	

PASTA SAUCE

This sauce will keep for up to 10 days in the refrigerator. The reason for adding the oregano and basil towards the end of cooking is that soft-leaved herbs can become very bitter if cooked for too long. This recipe freezes well. Fresh or tinned tomatoes may be used in this recipe.

onions, finely chopped	3 large	Sauté until soft, stirring
carrots, finely grated	2 medium	occasionally.
garlic, crushed	3 cloves	
olive oil	1 tablespoon	
mushrooms, finely chopped	250 g (½ lb)	Add, sauté on high heat for 5 minutes stirring continually.
tomatoes, peeled	1 kg (2 lb)	Remove seeds, chop flesh. Save any juice drips. Add to above.
red wine	½ cup	Add to above. Simmer for 30
tomato purée	1 cup	minutes, stirring occasionally.
bay leaf	1	Remove bay leaf.
sugar	2 teaspoons	
salt	1 teaspoon	
black pepper	½ teaspoon	
lemon rind strip	1.5 cm × 2.5 cm (2″ × 1″)	
oregano, fresh, finely chopped	2 teaspoons	Add. Simmer for a further 15
basil, fresh, finely chopped	1 tablespoon	minutes. Pour into hot, sterile jars. Seal.

PEANUT SAUCE (SAUS KACAY)

This Indonesian sauce may be served over hot or cold cooked vegetables or folded through pasta and sprinkled with chopped hard boiled eggs and serundeng (recipe follows). Children love this sauce if you keep the chilli content reasonably low. It will keep refrigerated for about one week.

peanut butter, smooth	4 tablespoons	Add the water a little at a time
water, warm	1 cup	until very smooth.
margarine	1 tablespoon	Sauté until transparent.
onion, finely chopped	1	
garlic clove, crushed	1	
chilli powder	1–2 teaspoons	Add, sauté 2 minutes more. Add all the above.
shrimp paste (optional)	tiny sliver	Chop the leaf in four pieces. Add all to above. Bring slowly to a boil, stirring continuously.
lemongrass (optional)	½ leaf	
salt	½ teaspoon	
soya sauce	2 teaspoons	
vinegar	1 teaspoon	
brown sugar	1 teaspoon	
coconut milk	½ cup	Add, stirring. Remove lemongrass.

PESTO

This paste will keep for one month in the refrigerator if covered with a layer of olive oil and sealed well. Serve it on steaks or folded through pasta or rice.

fresh basil leaves	1 cup packed	Blend together in a food processor or blender.
garlic cloves, peeled	4	
walnut pieces	½ cup	
olive or safflower oil	1 cup	Add slowly while blending.
parmesan, freshly grated	½ cup	Add, blend.
salt and black pepper	to taste	

PICKLES, CHUTNEYS & MUSTARDS

Eat, drink and love; the rest's not worth a fillip.
—Byron (1788–1824)

Pickles

SPICED CHERRIES

A very sophisticated pickled fruit. I like to take spiced cherries on picnics as they are an exciting and luxurious addition to the menu. Cherries don't have a very long season so make sure that you store enough for a year. Any cherries may be used but, in my opinion, the black cherries look and taste the best.

white wine vinegar	2 cups	Bring all to a boil in a non-aluminium saucepan. Take off heat and leave for 12 hours. Strain. Discard herb sprigs.
water	1 cup	
white sugar	200 g	
coriander seeds	20	
cinnamon stick, broken	1	
cloves, whole	12	
lemon or garden thyme	4 small sprigs	
fresh cherries with stalks	1 kg (2 lb)	Wash and dry. Layer the seeds and some fresh herb sprigs with the cherries in wide-mouthed jars.
brandy	3 tablespoons	Add to the vinegar. Fill the jars to cover the cherries. Seal.

SPICED PLUMS

The plums tend to shrink after a few days so it's good to have a spare jar for 'topping up' before you give the plums as a gift. This preserve keeps for a long time and shouldn't be used for about two months after making. The skins of the plums become quite tough but the delicious flesh is good with cold meats and meat pies, cheeses, and roasts.

Pre-heat oven to 120°C (250°F).

dark plums	2 kg (4 lb)	Prick plums with a fork. Put in a single layer in baking dishes with the remaining ingredients. Cover the dish. Bake for about ½–¾ of an hour until the plums have begun to soften. *Don't overcook.* Leave for about 12 hours.
soft brown sugar	1 kg (2 lb)	
water	1 cup	
malt vinegar	to cover	
cinnamon sticks	2 per jar	Drain the plums and arrange in jars with the other ingredients. Bring the liquid to the boil and simmer for 15 minutes. Fill the jars to cover the fruit. Seal.
cloves	4 per jar	
orange rind in strips	2 per jar	

WATERMELON PICKLE

This is a most delicious sweet pickle which goes well with cheeses, cold meats and also with curries as a side-dish. Unlike many recipes for this pickle I leave a little of the red flesh on the rind; it adds to the flavour and the appearance and doesn't affect the keeping qualities. Leave this pickle for at least two weeks before using.

watermelon rind	*500 g (1 lb)*	Leave a shaving of flesh on the rind, peel the tough skin off and cut into strips 7.5 cm (3″) long × 1¼ cm (½″) wide.
salt	*4 tablespoons*	Mix through rind.
water	*to cover*	Add. Stir well. Leave 12 hours. Drain. Rinse several times. Pat dry and put in a strong, non-aluminium pan.
water	*to cover*	Cover the rind. Bring to the boil. Simmer for 5 minutes. Drain.
sugar white wine vinegar cinnamon stick, broken mixed pickling spices	*2 cups* *1½ cups* *½* *2 teaspoons*	Bring to the boil in a non-aluminium pan. Simmer for 10 minutes. Strain. Pour over rind and simmer until rind is translucent and the syrup is thickened. Pack into hot sterile jars (see p.11). Cover closely with vinegar-proof lids.

PICKLED GHERKINS

The gherkins need to be kept for one week or so before using. They are best used within three months.

salt water gherkins	*¼ cup* *4 cups* *500 g (1 lb)*	Mix the water and salt until dissolved. Add the gherkins and leave for 12 hours, stirring often. Drain. Rinse several times.
fennel leaves coriander seeds dill seed peppercorns	*handful* *2 tablespoons* *2 teaspoons* *2 teaspoons*	Layer with the gherkins in a wide-mouthed jar.
white vinegar salt sugar	*2 cups* *2 teaspoons* *2 teaspoons*	Bring to the boil in a non-aluminium pan. Pour over the gherkins. Seal with a vinegar-proof lid.

PICKLED RED CABBAGE

Leave the cabbage for one week before using but don't store for more than three months or it loses the crunchy texture which is so appealing. One of my favourite 'comfort foods' as a child was a steaming mound of creamy mashed potatoes and red cabbage.

red cabbage	1	Remove outer leaves and core. Slice finely. Layer with cabbage in a bowl, press down with a weighted plate. Leave 24 hours. Wash under running water for several minutes. Drain and pat dry. Pack loosely in jars.
salt	2 cups	
spiced vinegar (see p.58)	3-4 cups	Pour over to cover cabbage. Seal with vinegar-proof lids.

GIARDINIERA—ITALIAN PICKLED VEGETABLES

The vegetables may be used as appetisers, in salads or with cheeses or cold meats.

small carrots	15	Peel, cut in thin 5 cm (2") strips.
celery	½ small bunch	String, slice in four lengthwise and then in 5 cm strips.
red capsicum	2	Remove seeds and stems. Cut into 2.5 cm (1") cubes.
green capsicum	2	
cauliflower	½	Break into tiny florets.
pickling onions	16	Peel.
salt	1½ cups	Dissolve together. Pour over the vegetables to cover (add more water if needed). Leave for 12 hours. Drain, rinse well. Drain well.
water	5 L (9 pints)	
white wine vinegar	8 cups	Bring to a boil in a non-aluminium pan, simmer for 5 minutes. Add vegetables and simmer for 5 minutes or until the vegetables are tender but still crisp. Pack the vegetables into very hot, wide-necked jars and fill with vinegar to 5 cm (2") from the top. Tap on a board to exclude air. Top up with 2.5 cm (1") olive oil and seal.
coriander seeds	1 tablespoon	
peppercorns	1 tablespoon	
dried chilli	2	
sugar, white	2 cups	

CHILLI PICKLED VEGETABLES

If you enjoy a hearty pickle there is a good chance that this chilli pickle will be a hit with you. It can be as hot as you like depending on the number of chillies used. It makes a good side-dish with Indian, Asian, and Mexican foods. The vegetables will keep for months if a layer of oil is poured over the top. (See p.9 for hints on handling chillies before making this recipe.)

chillies, green & red	9–12	Trim stalks, cut in half lengthwise. Seed and chop.
carrots	4 large	Cut into 2.5 cm (1") strips.
capsicums, red & green	2 of each	Cut into 1 cm (½") cubes.
onions	4	Slice thinly into half-moons.
French beans	250 g (½ lb)	Slice diagonally and thinly.
celery	4 stalks	
olive oil	6 tablespoons	Heat the oil—preferably in a wok. Stir-fry the above on a high heat, stirring constantly for about 5 minutes. Put all in a large bowl.
oregano, fresh, finely chopped	2 teaspoons	Put all in a pan. Bring to the boil.
thyme, fresh, finely chopped	2 teaspoons	Pour over the vegetables. Allow to
coriander seeds	1 teaspoon	cool. Bottle. Top up with a layer of
cumin seeds	½ teaspoon	olive oil, about 1 cm (½"). Seal
salt	4 teaspoons	with a vinegar-proof lid.
black pepper, cracked	1 teaspoon	
garlic, crushed	4 cloves	
sugar, dark brown	4 tablespoons	
cider vinegar	4 cups	

CHINESE PICKLED VEGETABLES

These vegetables are visually very attractive and taste as good as they look. They can be served as a side dish, with cheese and crackers, mixed in with green salads or as a salad on their own. Chinese vegetables will keep for up to four months if a good layer of oil is poured on top of the vegetables and they are stored in a cool dry area.

rice vinegar	4 cups	Bring to the boil.
water	2 cups	
salt	1 teaspoon	
sugar, white	2 teaspoons	
carrots cut in sticks	5	Add. Simmer for 6 minutes. Remove.

cauliflower, small florets	½ a head	Add. Simmer for 5 minutes. Remove.
celery, sliced diagonally	½ a head	Simmer for 4 minutes. Remove.
green beans, sliced diagonally	125 g (4 oz)	Simmer for 4 minutes. Remove.
onions, very small	125 g (4 oz)	Simmer for 4 minutes. Remove.
capsicums, red and green, cubed	½ each	Simmer for 4 minutes. Remove.
rice vinegar	4 cups	Add to the liquid in the pan. Bring to the boil.
capers peppercorns, mixed garlic, sliced	1 tablespoon 1 tablespoon 2 cloves	Using a wide-mouthed jar, layer the vegetables with these flavourings in an attractive pattern (you can mix them if you prefer). Pour the vinegar over to cover completely.
olive oil		Pour about 1 cm (½") on top to create an air seal.

PICKLED LEMONS

Pickled lemons are an elegant accompaniment to spicy food and rice, so can be served with Indian, Mexican, Middle Eastern, or Asian foods.

lemons, thin-skinned	2 kg (4 lb)	Freeze for 24 hours. Cut into quarters lengthwise, discard pips. Save all juice drips. Pack the fruit into wide-mouthed jars.
cooking salt turmeric cracked black pepper chilli powder white wine vinegar	½ cup 2 teaspoons 1 teaspoon ½ teaspoon 1 cup + extra	Mix together until salt is dissolved. Add a little more vinegar if necessary. Divide equally between the jars, top up with extra vinegar to cover the lemons. Seal with a vinegar-proof lid. Keep in a warm place for about 6 weeks, shake the jars daily. After 6 weeks the lemons can be moved to the storeroom where they need to mature for a further 6 months before use.

Chutneys

SYLVIA'S DATE AND APPLE CHUTNEY

This is a sweet, delicious chutney. It isn't cooked and doesn't have long keeping qualities and would need to be kept refrigerated. It's quick and easy to make.

cooking apples, peeled, cored	500 g (1 lb)	Mince, put in a large bowl.
onions, peeled	500 g (1 lb)	
sultanas	500 g (1 lb)	
dates, dried, stoned	500 g (1 lb)	
raw brown sugar	500 g (1 lb)	Add to above. Mix well.
salt	1 teaspoon	
ginger powder	1 teaspoon	
cinnamon, ground	1 teaspoon	
black pepper	pinch	
spiced malt vinegar	2½ cups	Pour over. Leave for 24 hours, stirring occasionally. Fill jars. Seal with vinegar-proof lids. Leave for a few days before eating.

DATE AND APRICOT CHUTNEY

Another delightful sweet chutney using dried fruits. This recipe was given to me by an old woman with very young tastes.

dried apricots	500 g (1 lb)	Cut in quarters. Cover with cold water and soak for 6 hours.
dried, stoned dates, chopped	1 kg (2 lb)	Put all with apricots in a non-aluminium pan. Stir well to mix.
garlic, crushed	2 cloves	
cooking apples, peeled, chopped	2	
raisins	500 g (1 lb)	
glacé ginger, finely chopped	220 g (7 oz)	
salt	2 teaspoons	
cinnamon	½ teaspoon	
light brown sugar	3 cups	
white vinegar	to cover	Pour over above. Cook very slowly till thick, about 1½–2 hours. Pot and seal with vinegar-proof lids. Leave for one week before using.

INDIAN 'CHATNI'

This chutney will keep for at least one year if correctly covered. It is a *very* hot and spicy chutney which may have its fire dampened down by using less chilli and mustard.

malt vinegar	*4 cups*	Peel, core and slice apples. Put
cooking apples	*500 g (1 lb)*	all into a non-aluminium pan.
onions, chopped	*250 g (½ lb)*	Cook until very soft. Sieve or
light brown sugar	*2½ cups*	blend until smooth.
garlic, crushed	*4 cloves*	
salt	*½ cup*	
ground almonds	*1 cup*	Mix all well. Add to the above.
sultanas, chopped finely	*250 g (½ lb)*	Cover and leave for 24 hours,
mustard powder	*6 tablespoons*	stirring occasionally. If the mixture
chilli powder	*5 tablespoons*	feels too dry then more malt
ground ginger	*125 g (¼ lb)*	vinegar may be added. Put into
		small jars and cover closely with
		vinegar-proof lids.

SAMBAL PEDIS (HOT FRIED CHILLI CHUTNEY)

This recipe was given to me by Fee Le Faucheur and it is Indonesian in origin. She tells me that a little coconut cream added before serving gives an even better flavour.

oil	*1 cup*	Blend all together to a coarse
red chillies, chopped	*12*	paste. Put in a frypan and cook,
brown onions, chopped	*4*	stirring for 10 minutes.
garlic cloves	*8*	
macadamia nuts, chopped	*12*	
dark brown sugar	*2 tablespoons*	Cut the lemongrass leaves into
white vinegar	*2 tablespoons*	5 cm (1") pieces. Add all to the
salt	*1 teaspoon*	frypan and continue frying and
lemongrass leaf (optional)	*2 leaves*	stirring until the moisture has
		dried up. Spoon into hot jars with
		vinegar-proof lids.

PREVIOUS PAGE
A dinner basket might include chicken liver pâté with Cointreau, a cheese ball, Melba toast, pesto with noodles, mixed devilled nuts, Italian herb dressing, Middle-Eastern fruit salad, fennel seeds, and rosemary digestive wine (see also p.132).

OPPOSITE
An after-dinner basket might include frosted dates, chocolate ginger, kirsch and almond dates, marzipan nut balls, spicy peps, grapefruit candy, spiced cherries, and a selection of liqueurs (see also p.132).

MANGO CHUTNEY

It's not always possible to buy fresh mangoes so here is a good recipe which uses tinned mangoes.

tinned mango	2 × 425 g	Drain. Chop into large pieces.
onions, chopped	2	Mix all in a non-aluminium bowl.
tomatoes, peeled, chopped	4	Stand for 12 hours. Stir
apples, peeled, cored, chopped	3	occasionally. Pour into a non-
raisins	½ cup	aluminium saucepan. Bring to a
ginger root, crushed	1 teaspoon	boil. Reduce the heat and simmer,
garlic, crushed	2 cloves	uncovered, until thick for 1½–2
salt	1 teaspoon	hours. Pour into hot sterile jars.
curry powder	1 tablespoon	Seal.
dark brown sugar	1 cup	
malt vinegar	1½ cups	
lemon juice	½ cup	

Mustards

It is a mistake to assume that all mustards are hot. The addition of either hot water or vinegar to ground mustard seed will create a milder mustard as the enzyme action is inhibited. My father used to mix yellow mustard powder with cold water to use on his Sunday roast beef, and I remember the tears and the pain when I was rash enough to try some! For those of you who dislike very pungent condiments I have included several mustards, some of which are sweet, some mild, or tasty without much heat.

I give gifts of sets of four mustards to please all tastes. Mustards need time to mature, the initial taste is often harsh and two to three weeks are needed to develop the true flavour. These mustards keep well in a cool dark place but need refrigeration once they have been opened. Check the mustards from time to time and thin with vinegar or wine if they are getting too thick.

MEXICAN MUSTARD

This mustard can be as mild or as hot as you choose depending on the amount of chilli powder you use.

white mustard seed	6 teaspoons	Grind to the texture you like.
black mustard seed	3 teaspoons	Avoid leaving it too coarse.
coriander seed	6 teaspoons	

water	5 tablespoons	Add and let stand for 2 hours.
white vinegar	3 tablespoons	
soya sauce	1 teaspoon	
dark brown sugar	3 rounded teaspoons	Add and mix well. Leave in a covered container for 24 hours, stirring occasionally. If the mixture becomes too thick it may be thinned with more vinegar and water. Store in small jars.
plain flour	2 level tablespoons	
cumin seed, ground	1 level teaspoon	
chilli powder	a dash	

HERB MUSTARD 1

This is a mild mustard, particularly good with cheese and cold chicken. The herbs may be varied depending on availability and preference.

black mustard seed	1 tablespoon	Grind to a coarse flour.
white mustard seed	1 tablespoon	
plain flour	3 tablespoons	
celery salt	½ teaspoon	
chives, finely chopped	1 tablespoon	Add to above. Mix well.
parsley, finely chopped	1 tablespoon	
sage, finely chopped	1 teaspoon	
olive oil	¼ cup	Mix together very well. Mix slowly with above. Leave in a covered bowl for 24 hours. Stir often. Pot.
sweet sherry	1 teaspoon	
cider vinegar	¼ cup	
honey	2 teaspoons	

HERB MUSTARD 2

mustard powder	1 cup	Blend all until very fine.
parsley, fresh	2 tablespoons	
coriander, fresh	2 tablespoons	
ground cumin	½ tablespoon	
ground coriander	1 teaspoon	
olive oil	¼ cup	Mix together then blend well with above. Leave in a covered bowl for 24 hours, stirring often. Add more vinegar if too dry. Pot. Cover closely.
cider vinegar	½ cup	
sugar	1 tablespoon	
plain flour	½ cup	

GARLIC MUSTARD 1

garlic, minced	*2 cloves*	Combine all in a bowl. Cover and
onions, large, chopped	*1*	stand for about 24 hours. Stir
white wine vinegar	*1 cup*	often. Strain. Reserve vinegar.
basil, chopped	*1 teaspoon*	
mustard powder	*⅔ cup*	Mix together and slowly add
plain flour	*1 teaspoon*	enough of the white wine vinegar
honey	*1 tablespoon*	to make a smooth thin cream.
paprika	*½ teaspoon*	Bring the remaining vinegar to
		the boil and pour slowly onto the
		mustard, stirring all the time. Put
		into a small saucepan and simmer
		for 6 minutes. Stir continuously.
		Cool slightly.
olive oil	*1½ tablespoons*	Add. Mix well. Cover and leave
		for 24 hours, stirring often. Spoon
		into small jars and cover with
		close-fitting lids.

GARLIC MUSTARD 2

mustard powder	*½ cup*	Combine all. Leave in a covered
garlic cloves, crushed	*4*	container for 24 hours, stirring
salt	*1 teaspoon*	occasionally. Add more vinegar if
cider vinegar	*½ cup*	necessary. Pot.
olive oil	*2 tablespoons*	
honey	*3 teaspoons*	

PEPPERCORN MUSTARD

mustard powder	5 tablespoons	Mix together and leave for 30 minutes.
cold water	3 tablespoons	
white wine vinegar	¼ cup	
olive oil	2 teaspoons	
green peppercorns, tinned	1 tablespoon	Mix well with above. Leave for 24 hours. Adjust liquid, adding more white wine vinegar if too dry. Spoon into small pots, seal.
salt	1 teaspoon	
honey	1 tablespoon	
mixed spice	½ teaspoon	

PINK PEPPERCORN MUSTARD

pink peppercorns	3 tablespoons	Grind to the texture you like, put in a mixing bowl.
white mustard seeds	6 tablespoons	
dry white wine	3 tablespoons	Add. Mix and leave to soak for one hour.
allspice	½ teaspoon	Blend with above until well mixed. Add more white wine if the mixture seems too dry. Leave in a covered bowl for 24 hours, stirring often before potting.
white wine vinegar	¼ cup	
honey	2 tablespoons	
salt	1–2 teaspoons	

MILD MUSTARD

white wine vinegar	1 cup	
cornflour	2 heaped tablespoons	Mix all well with a little of the vinegar. Bring the remaining vinegar to the boil, add to the mixture while stirring. Cook in a small non-aluminium pan until thickened. Cover and leave for 24 hours, stirring often. Add more white wine vinegar if needed. Pot.
chilli powder	small pinch	
mustard powder	3 heaped tablespoons	
turmeric	1 teaspoon	
nutmeg	pinch	
salt	1 teaspoon	
honey	1–2 teaspoons	

HOT HORSERADISH MUSTARD

white mustard seed	5 tablespoons	Grind to a coarse powder. Place in a blender.
horseradish, grated	1 tablespoon	Add and blend until smooth. Spoon into small jars. Seal.
olive oil	¼ cup	
cider vinegar	½ cup	
honey	2 teaspoons	
salt	1 teaspoon	
garlic clove	1	
lemon zest (p.14)	1 teaspoon	

VINEGARS, OILS & DRESSINGS

A gourmet is just a glutton with brains.
—P.W. Haberman, jun. (1905–71)

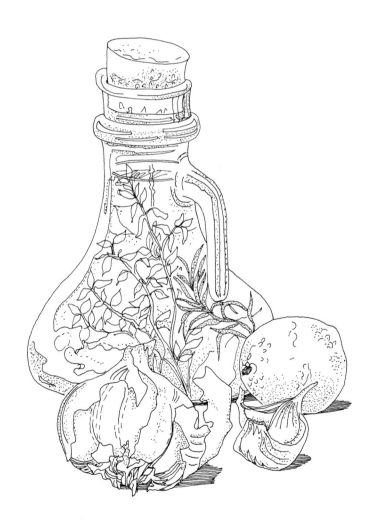

I make most of my flavoured vinegars and oils in the summer when the herbs are at their best. They then have the flavour and scent of summer all winter.

It is simpler to have a range of flavoured vinegars and oils ready-made than to have to add the flavourings when you may need to prepare food quickly. These recipes keep well out of the refrigerator unless the weather or room is hot. When giving herb vinegars as gifts you will need to put fresh herbs in the bottle at the last minute as the vinegar strips the colour fairly quickly. Dressings containing eggs should be refrigerated and are at their best for about three weeks to a month.

It's important to use very good quality vinegar for these recipes. Cheap or malt vinegars are too harsh and the flavour of the added ingredients is largely lost.

Vinegars

LEMON VINEGAR

This vinegar is delicious in dressings, marinades or sprinkled on fish before or after cooking.

white wine vinegar	2 cups	Bottle. Leave for one week. Strain
lemon juice	2 lemons	through coffee filter paper.
peppercorns, black	8	Re-bottle and add a long twisted strip of lemon peel to each bottle.

PINK VINEGAR

A lovely pink colour makes this a very attractive gift as well as a practical one. It can be used in any dish where the flavours of onion, garlic, pepper and vinegar are needed.

white wine vinegar	2 cups	Heat to blood heat in a non-aluminium pan.
garlic, finely chopped	2 cloves	Add to the vinegar. Pour into a
red onion, finely chopped	1 large	large jar with a well-fitting
red peppercorns	1 tablespoon	vinegar-proof lid. Leave in a warm place for one week, shaking the jar often. Strain well. Bottle.
red peppercorns	1 teaspoon	Add. Seal with vinegar-proof lids or caps.

HONEYED HERB VINEGAR

cider vinegar	5 cups	Simmer together in a non-
garlic, sliced	2 cloves	aluminium saucepan for 6–7
honey	½ cup	minutes. Cool. Strain very well
oregano, dried	1 tablespoon	through cheesecloth (p.9). Bottle.
peppermint, dried	2 teaspoons	Add a sprig of thyme to each
thyme, dried	2 teaspoons	bottle. Seal with vinegar-proof lids
chives, fresh, chopped	2 teaspoons	or caps. Mature for 3 weeks
		before using.

HERB VINEGAR

Use your own favourite mix of herbs for this recipe. A good one is thyme, savoury, basil, oregano, and a bay leaf.

herbs, fresh, chopped	1 cup	Mix together in a jar. Seal and
cider vinegar	5 cups	leave in a warm place for 2 weeks,
		shaking often. Strain well. Bottle.
		Add two or three sprigs of herb to
		each bottle. Seal with vinegar-
		proof lids or caps.

TARRAGON VINEGAR

Absolutely my favourite vinegar on almost everything. Use fresh tarragon and the finest vinegar to achieve a superb flavour. If however you can only get dried tarragon it's better to use this than to not have tarragon vinegar.

tarragon leaves, chopped	1 cup	Method as herb vinegar, above.
white wine vinegar	3 cups	

'PRANCING PONY' VINEGAR

We often used this vinegar blend at our restaurant 'The Prancing Pony'. It gives an unusual flavour to green salads and is an excellent base for a herb marinade.

lemon thyme, fresh, chopped	4 tablespoons	Method the same as herb vinegar
thyme, fresh, chopped	4 tablespoons	(see above).
sage, fresh, chopped	2 tablespoons	
garlic, sliced	2 cloves	
cider vinegar	3 cups	

HORSERADISH OR GINGER VINEGAR

This is a way of providing flavoured vinegar and also storing horseradish or ginger. Either of these vinegars gives extra flavour to plain foods, salads, marinades or other dishes where these flavours are appreciated.

ginger root scrubbbed, cut into 2½ cm (1") cubes *or* horseradish root, scrubbed and grated (see p.10) cider vinegar	Put the prepared root into wide-mouthed jars. Add the vinegar to cover 2.5 cm (1") above the root. The vinegar may be used within a few days and the jar topped up with fresh vinegar.

SPICED VINEGAR

This is used when making pickles, chutneys or some marinated vegetables. It's useful to keep some on hand as it will keep for months and saves time when you need to make a gift. It is possible to buy spiced vinegar but homemade vinegar is far superior to most bought varieties.

malt vinegar	*8 cups*	Bring all to a boil in a non-aluminium pan. Cover and leave for 24 hours. Strain (see p.11). Bottle and cap with vinegar-proof lids.
sugar	*1 cup*	
salt	*2 teaspoons*	
cinnamon stick, broken	*6 cm (2½")*	
allspice berries, bruised	*14*	
black peppercorns, bruised	*16*	
ginger, crushed	*5 cm (2")*	
cloves, bruised	*6*	
mace	*2 teaspoons*	
celery seeds	*2 teaspoons*	

Oils

I have three bottles of oil near my stove, these are chili, mixed herb, and garlic–peppercorn. By using these oils I am able to baste, sauté, season or make dressings with the time-saving of only using one step to achieve the oiling and flavouring.

HERB OIL

		Half-fill a jar with the herbs.
tarragon, fresh chopped	*½ cup*	
thyme, fresh	*¼ cup*	
chives, chopped	*¼ cup*	
celery seed, crushed	*2 teaspoons*	
olive oil		Fill the jar with a mixture of the two oils. Cover. Leave in a warm place for two weeks, shaking the jar often. Strain and re-bottle.
safflower oil		

CHILLI OIL 1

Don't treat this oil lightly—it's a good servant but a cruel master! If sautéeing, mix it with plain oil. Add in very small amounts to dips, dressings, and marinades (see p.9 for hints on chillies).

		Heat till quite hot.
safflower oil	*2 cups*	
dried chillies, chopped	*½ cup*	Add all to the hot oil. Stand overnight. Strain through double cheesecloth (see p.9). Pour into bottles. Seal well. Add 1 chilli to each bottle before giving as a gift.
chilli powder	*1 teaspoon*	
ginger, crushed	*¼ cup*	
black peppercorns, bruised	*24*	
garlic, crushed	*6 cloves*	
onion, chopped	*1 medium*	

CHILLI OIL 2

A simpler oil for those who want only chilli flavour. Removing the seeds results in a milder oil as the seeds are the hottest part. Cutting down on the number of chillies merely reduces the flavour. The oil will keep for about three months.

		Slit in half, lengthwise. Remove seeds if you wish. Put in a large, screw-topped jar.
green chillies	*2*	
red chillies	*1*	
virgin olive oil	*2 cups*	Warm, pour over chillies.
chilli powder	*1 teaspoon*	Add. Seal. Leave one week to mature. Strain and bottle. Add one green and one red chilli to the bottle before giving as a gift.

GARLIC OIL

This is a very useful oil as garlic flavour is needed in so many dishes. If you intend to store the oil in the refrigerator it is best to use safflower oil, but if (like me) you want to keep it near the stove, use virgin olive oil—the greener the better.

oil	4 cups	Put all in a screw-topped jar.
garlic cloves, sliced	8	Leave for one week in a warm place. Strain (use the garlic for cooking). Bottle. Add 3 fresh whole garlic cloves to each bottle.

Dressings

BASIC MAYONNAISE

This mayonnaise allows you to make many wonderful varieties of dressings.

One of my favourite additions to this mayonnaise is yoghurt. I make a very thick consistency with the oil and thin down with yoghurt. This makes a tangy, lower calorie dressing.

egg yolks	4	Place all into the bowl of a
French mustard	2 teaspoons	blender and beat until well
salt	1 teaspoon	blended.
pepper	½ teaspoon	
sugar (optional)	1 teaspoon	
white wine vinegar	3 teaspoons	
olive oil	2 cups (approx)	With the blender running slowly, drizzle the oil in a thin stream until about half has been used.
lemon juice	2 teaspoons	Add while beating, continue to add the oil until the desired thickness is achieved.

TARTARE SAUCE

basic mayonnaise (see above)	1 cup	Mix all well together. Pack in a
capers, chopped	2 teaspoons	jar with a tight-fitting, vinegar-
herbs, fresh, chopped	2 teaspoons	proof lid. Store in the refrigerator.
egg, hard-boiled, sieved	1	

AVOCADO MAYONNAISE

This is a lovely and unusual mayonnaise. It is suitable for serving with most salads and will store in the refrigerator for about a month.

avocado	*1*	Mash till smooth.
basic mayonnaise (see above)	*½ cup*	Mix well with above. Spoon into small jars. Refrigerate.
lemon juice	*2 tablespoons*	
sour cream	*2 tablespoons*	
fresh chives, finely chopped	*1 teaspoon*	

TOMATO MAYONNAISE

basic mayonnaise (see above)	*1 cup*	Mix all well together. Spoon into a jar with a well-fitting vinegar-proof lid. Store in the refrigerator.
fresh basil, chopped	*1 teaspoon*	
cream	*1 tablespoon*	
tomato sauce	*2 tablespoons*	

GREEN HERB MAYONNAISE

This mayonnaise looks as good as it tastes. The yoghurt gives a lovely tang. The flavour of fresh herbs is much better than dried herbs in this recipe and they give a better flavour and texture. I find a blender to be indispensable for making emulsions of this type as there is then little possibility of the mixture curdling—a real problem when you have to hand-beat.

cider vinegar	*2 tablespoons*	Put all in a blender and zoom for about 10 seconds.
egg yolk	*1*	
whole egg	*1*	
French mustard	*2 teaspoons*	
basil	*2 tablespoons*	Finely chop the herbs. Add to the blender and zoom for a further 5 seconds.
oregano	*2 tablespoons*	
chives	*1 tablespoon*	
parsley	*1 tablespoon*	
salt	*to taste*	
black pepper	*to taste*	
sugar	*1 teaspoon*	
olive oil	*1 cup (approx)*	Add to the switched-on blender in a slow stream until the mixture is *very* thick and smooth. Add more oil if needed.
yoghurt	*¼ cup*	With the blender still running, add the yoghurt slowly. Pot. Store in the refrigerator.

GREEN GODDESS DRESSING

Another green and gorgeous mayonnaise. This one is a little easier than the previous recipes because you start with ready-made mayonnaise.

basic mayonnaise (see p.60)	1 cup	Mix well together in a bowl.
yoghurt	½ cup	
sour cream	¼ cup	
parsley, fresh, chopped	4 tablespoons	These herbs need to be chopped
spring onions, chopped	¼ cup	very finely either by hand or in a
fennel leaves, chopped	2 tablespoons	blender with a chopping blade.
mint, chopped	2 teaspoons	Add to above.
lemon juice	1 tablespoon	Mix with all of above until very
garlic powder	¼ teaspoon	smooth. Store in a covered jar in
salt & pepper	to taste	the refrigerator.
paprika	⅛ teaspoon	
sugar	1 teaspoon	

CREAMY EGG VINAIGRETTE

virgin olive oil	1 cup	Shake all together until thick and
tarragon vinegar	⅓ cup	creamy.
egg yolk	1	
sugar	2 teaspoons	
dry English mustard	2 teaspoons	
salt	good pinch	
black pepper	good pinch	

SEAFOOD DRESSING

After trying this recipe you won't ever got back to the tasteless, bottled dressings which pass for seafood dressings. This dressing also tastes particularly good with avocado.

basic mayonnaise (see p.60)	1 cup	Mix all well together. Store in the
double cream	¼ cup	refrigerator.
tomato ketchup	¼ cup	
tabasco sauce	to taste	
lemon juice	1 teaspoon	
salt	pinch	
pepper	pinch	

A SALAD DRESSING

To make this condiment your poet begs
The pounded yolks of two hard boiled eggs.
Two boiled potatoes, pressed through kitchen sieve
Smoothness and softness to the salad give.
Let onion atoms lurk within the bowl
And, half suspected, animate the whole.
Of morduant mustard add a single spoon.
Distrust the condiment that bites too soon;
But deem it not, though man of herbs, a fault,
To add a double quantity of salt;
Four times the spoon with oil from Lucca Brown,
And twice with vinegar procured from town;
And, lastly o'er the flavoured compound toss
A magic soupcon of anchovy sauce.
Oh, green and glorious! Oh, herbaceous treat!
'Twould tempt the dying anchorite to eat:
Back to the world he'd turn his fleeting soul
And plunge his fingers in the salad bowl!
Serenely full, the epicure would say,
'Fate cannot harm me, I have dined today'

Rev. Sydney Smith
(1771–1845)

(This charming recipe doesn't keep well because of the potato in it but it would make a lovely gift if the poem was written on a card and attached to the neck of the jar.)

ROQUEFORT DRESSING

This dressing will keep for up to three weeks if refrigerated. The flavour is wonderful and gives a lift to a plain salad.

roquefort cheese	60 g (2 oz)	Mix all in blender until very smooth.
sour cream	¼ cup	
white wine vinegar	2 tablespoons	
egg yolk	1	
chilli powder	pinch	
French mustard	½ teaspoon	
dried tarragon	1 teaspoon	
salt	½ teaspoon	
sugar	½ teaspoon	
cracked black pepper	¼ teaspoon	
olive oil		With the blender running, add the oil in a slow stream until the required consistency is reached.

ITALIAN HERB DRESSING

The following recipe could be given as a dry-mix, attractively packaged with a card attached giving instructions for making the finished dressing. The herbs are all dried and rubbed to the texture of tea-leaves. An appropriate gift to give with the herbs would be a beautiful vinaigrette bottle.

oregano	1½ cups	Mix all well together.
basil	1 cup	
paprika	2 tablespoons	
garlic powder	2 tablespoons	
onion powder	½ cup	
dry mustard	2 tablespoons	
salt	2 teaspoons	
cracked black pepper	1 tablespoon	
olive oil	1½ cups	Combine, add 2 tablespoons of the dry-mix. Shake well. Stand for at least 2 hours before using.
white wine vinegar	½ cup	

ESCABECHE DRESSING

This is an adaptation of an old recipe. A dash of this sauce will give a lift to bland foods or to soups and stews. It may be kept on the table as a condiment but needs a tiny opening in the bottle neck as a little goes a long way. It is excellent sprinkled on fish either at the table or used as a marinade, sprinkling a little over the fish about one hour before cooking.

wine vinegar	3 cups	Bring to a boil in a non-aluminium saucepan.
lemon zest (see p.14)	1 lemon	Add all. Simmer for 10 minutes. Allow to cool. Strain through double cheesecloth (see p.9). Bottle. Seal with vinegar-proof lids or caps.
ginger root, crushed finely	2 tablespoons	
coriander seeds, bruised	2 tablespoons	
horseradish root, grated	1 teaspoon	
chilli powder	½ teaspoon	
garlic cloves, crushed finely	8	
large onions, sliced	4	

OPPOSITE
A picnic basket might include pickled eggs, cheesy water-biscuits, pickled mushrooms, spicy peps, watermelon pickle, lemon cordial and figs in port (see also p.132).

OVERLEAF
A gourmet cook's basket might include candied peel, vanilla essence, citrus powder, Mexican seasoning, garam masala, Worcestershire sauce, herbs, pickled nasturtium seeds, and a selection of oils and vinegars (see also p.133).

ROUILLE

A gorgeous orange dressing which doubles as a dip. Best used within two weeks of making and needs storing in the refrigerator.

garlic	2 cloves	Mash to a paste in a mortar and
salt	2 teaspoons	pestle.
basic mayonnaise (see p.60)	1 cup	Add, leave for 30 minutes.
mustard, French	1 tablespoon	Add and mix well. Store in the
paprika	1 tablespoon	refrigerator in a jar with a well-
fresh orange juice	½ cup	fitting lid.
brandy	4 tablespoons	
sugar	1 teaspoon	
white wine vinegar	2 tablespoons	

HERB VINAIGRETTE 1

These two vinaigrettes are adaptations of the traditional recipe. Both taste fresh and delicious on plain green salads and, if refrigerated, keep well for several weeks.

The herbs should be fresh and finely chopped.

virgin olive oil	1 cup	Finely chop the onions and the
garlic clove, crushed	1	herbs. Put all in a jar with a well-
spring onions	1 cup	fitting lid. Shake until well
parsley	½ cup	blended and thick.
basil	1 tablespoon	
oregano	¼ cup	
French mustard	1 teaspoon	
lemon juice	2 tablespoons	
white wine vinegar	2 tablespoons	
salt & pepper	to taste	
honey	1 tablespoon	

HERB VINAIGRETTE 2

white wine vinegar	⅓ cup	Put all in a screw-topped jar.
olive oil	1 cup	Shake well to blend. Decant into
parsley, fresh, chopped	3 teaspoons	an ornamental bottle to give as a
garlic, crushed	½ clove	gift.
spring onion, finely chopped	1	
French mustard	1 teaspoon	
salt	to taste	
black pepper	to taste	

SEASONINGS & ESSENCES

After a good dinner, one can forgive anybody, even one's own relations.
—Oscar Wilde (1854–1900)

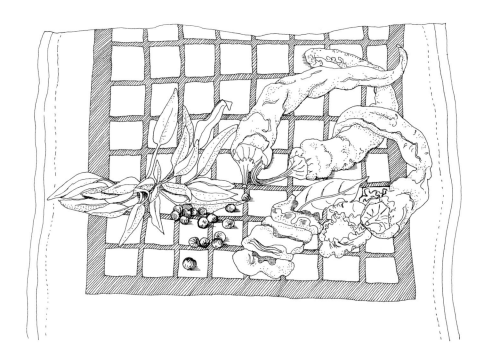

Seasonings

For a keen cook there is no more exciting gift than freshly made flavourings and seasonings—particularly if they are new to her (or him!) and you include a recipe for their use. There is no comparison between homemade, fresh, aroma-filled spices and the staler, commercial variety.

The seeds can be 'roasted' under the grill or in a pan on the stove top rather than in the oven but greater care needs to be taken not to burn them. The finished products need to be stored in tightly capped small jars in a cool dark place to retain their freshness for as long as possible.

HOT CURRY POWDER

cumin seeds	*1 tablespoon*	Roast all the seeds separately until
fenugreek seeds	*1 tablespoon*	fragrant. Take great care not to
yellow mustard seeds	*2 teaspoons*	burn them. Allow to cool. Grind
black peppercorns	*1 tablespoon*	to a powder.
coriander seeds	*6 tablespoons*	
poppy seeds	*1 teaspoon*	
cinnamon, ground	*3 tablespoons*	Mix well with the above. Sieve.
turmeric, ground	*4 tablespoons*	See the beginning of this section
ginger, ground	*3 teaspoons*	for storage hints.
chillies, dried, ground	*4 tablespoons*	

MILD CURRY POWDER

cloves, whole	*4 teaspoons*	Roast all separately until fragrant.
cinnamon stick	*6 × 7.5 cm (3″)*	Allow to cool. Grind to a powder.
black peppercorns	*¼ cup*	
cardamom seeds (not pods)	*2 tablespoons*	
mace	*2 tablespoons*	Grind. Add to above. Sieve and store in a cool, dark place.

CURRY PASTE

This is a useful curry paste for busy people as there is no grinding to do. To use this paste, add 1 tablespoon to 500 g (1 lb) of meat or vegetables. If stored correctly the paste will keep for months.

coriander, ground	*1 cup*	Sieve all together into a bowl.
mustard powder	*2 tablespoons*	
chilli powder	*1 tablespoon*	
cumin, ground	*3 tablespoons*	
salt	*2 tablespoons*	
chickpea flour	*¼ cup*	
black pepper, ground	*1 tablespoon*	
garlic, crushed finely	*2 tablespoons*	Add to above and mix with
ginger, fresh, grated finely	*1½ tablespoons*	enough malt vinegar to make a
malt vinegar		smooth purée.
butter	*¼ cup*	Heat in a pan. Add all
oil	*¼ cup*	ingredients. Cook, stirring constantly on a low heat until the oil separates out and the spices are fragrant. Cool before bottling.

GARAM MASALA

This mixture adds fragrance and flavour to a dish without having the heat of a curry powder. There are many recipes for garam masala but this one is a particular favourite of mine—I have been using it for about 30 years!

black peppercorns	*6 tablespoons*	Roast all separately till fragrant.
fennel seeds	*2 tablespoons*	Cool. Grind and sieve. Store in an
blade mace	*1 tablespoon*	airtight jar in a cool, dark place.
cloves, whole	*1 tablespoon*	
cardamom seeds	*2 tablespoons*	
cinnamon stick	*6 × 5 cm (2")*	
caraway seeds	*3 tablespoons*	

MEXICAN SEASONING

Use this in re-fried beans, salsa, guacamole or in any dish where you want a Mexican flavour.

chilli powder	*1½ tablespoons*	Mix all well. Store in airtight
cumin, ground	*6 tablespoons*	containers in a cool, dark place.
coriander seeds, ground	*6 tablespoons*	
garlic powder (not salt)	*2 tablespoons*	
onion powder	*1 tablespoon*	
paprika	*2 tablespoons*	

ALL-PURPOSE HERB SEASONING

This dried herb mix is useful to have in the winter when fresh herbs are not available.

parsley	*8 tablespoons*	Grind all to a coarse powder.
thyme	*4 tablespoons*	
oregano	*4 tablespoons*	
lemon thyme	*1 tablespoon*	
paprika	*1 tablespoon*	
lemon peel, dried, ground	*1 tablespoon*	Add. Mix well. Store in airtight
garlic powder (not salt)	*1 tablespoon*	jars in a cool, dark place.
onion powder	*2 teaspoons*	
celery seeds, ground	*1 tablespoon*	

YESAME POWDER

A delicious, healthy substitute for salt. A very good gift for those health-conscious people. I specify Healtheries yeast *flakes* (not powder) because these are not as bitter as many of the brewers' yeasts. If you can't buy this brand ask your health food shop to suggest a mild yeast. The mixture is naturally salty and may be used instead of salt at the table, in soups, casseroles, and sandwiches. My grandchildren became addicted to this powder but reported that it didn't taste so good on ice-cream!

sesame seeds, roast, ground	1 cup	Grind the seeds with some of the yeast and then mix all together. Store in an airtight container in the refrigerator.
Healtheries yeast *flakes*	2 cups	

COCONUT SPRINKLE (SERUNDENG)

Stored in the refrigerator in a covered container, this will keep for six to eight weeks. I use it over vegetables, pasta, scrambled eggs, and in sandwiches.

Preheat oven to 150°C (300°F). Roasting tins needed.

peanuts, blanched, chopped	1½ cups	Roast till golden brown, leave to cool.
beef stock cube	1	Dissolve together.
hot water	2 tablespoons	
desiccated coconut	2 cups	Mix all very thoroughly (not the peanuts). Put into a baking tin.
salt & pepper	shake	
sugar	1 teaspoon	
onion, grated	1	
garlic clove, crushed	1	
coriander, ground	2 teaspoons	
lemon juice	1 teaspoon	Mix together, drizzle over the above. Mix well. Cook until the coconut is golden brown. Add the peanuts. Spread in a single layer to cool.
safflower oil	¼ cup	
sesame oil	2 teaspoons	

DRIED CITRUS POWDER

Dried, powdered peel adds wonderful flavour to cakes, pikelets, biscuits, puddings, and crepes. It has the advantage of costing nothing to make. Every time you need the flesh of an orange, mandarin, grapefruit or lemon, peel first very thinly avoiding the white pith. Leave the strips in a warm, dry, clean place until they are brittle. Grind to a powder, sieve and store in small jars in a cool, dark place.

Essences

ESSENCE OF VANILLA

It may seem pointless to make your own essence when the commercial variety is readily available. However, the homemade essence is so superior in strength that much less is needed and the flavour is wonderful.

vanilla pods	*4*	Cut into very small pieces. Put in a jar with the brandy. Seal tightly. Shake several times a week. Leave for two months before using. Strain before decanting into tiny bottles.
brandy	*2 cups*	

CELERY ESSENCE

This essence is made from the seeds of the celeriac plant. These seeds are readily available as 'celery seeds' from health food stores. The essence is very strong and only a few drops are needed to give a good celery flavour. The essence keeps indefinitely if correctly stored.

celery seeds	*6 tablespoons*	Bruise lightly (see p.9). Put in a jar.
brandy	*1½ cups*	Add. Seal the jar. Leave for 2 weeks, shaking daily. Strain. Pour into tiny bottles. Store in a cool, dark place.

FLAVOURED SUGAR

Oranges, lemons or mandarins may be used for this recipe. As the peel is the only part of the fruit which is used this makes a very economical gift. Use the sugar in pikelets, over sweet pancakes, in cakes or biscuits. Scrub the fruit thoroughly, peel thinly. Leave for 24 hours to partially dry. Layer the strips in a jar with white sugar always making the last layer sugar. Tap the jar base firmly several times on a wooden board to settle the sugar between the peel. Keep layering over a period of time until the jar is full. Seal the jar with a well-fitting lid. Leave for three weeks. Take out the peel and pack the sugar in ornamental jars with a swing tag giving suggestions for use.

Sweet Gifts

He looked up at his clock, which had stopped at five minutes to eleven some weeks ago.
'Nearly eleven o'clock,' said Pooh happily. 'You're just in time for a little smackerel of something...'

—A.A. Milne (1882–1956)

CAKES

SPICY GINGERBREAD

This is my mother's recipe for gingerbread and I love it—probably because of the memories
it evokes of my mother's kitchen with warm smells and warmer feelings.

Preheat the oven to 160°C (300°F). Grease and flour two small loaf tins, approximately
13 cm × 23 cm (5″ × 9″).

butter	320 g (10 oz)	Melt slowly to dissolve sugar.
sugar, soft, dark brown	320 g (10 oz)	Bring to the boil. Simmer 1-2
black treacle	320 g (10 oz)	minutes. Cool.
glacé ginger, chopped	¼ cup	Add to cooled mixture. Mix well.
mixed peel	¼ cup	
eggs, beaten	3	
milk	1½ cups	Mix together. Bring to blood heat.
sodium bicarbonate	3 level teaspoons	Add to above.
flour, plain	3 cups	Sieve together into a large bowl.
ground ginger	3 level tablespoons	Make a well in the centre. Add all
cinnamon	4 level teaspoons	above. Mix well but gently. Bake for 1-1½ hours (see p.9 for cake testing).

PANFORTE DI SIENA

This recipe was given to me by an Italian friend who tells me that it is eaten as a Christmas cake in Italy. It is a rich, solid cake (*panforte* means 'strong bread') which may be eaten at any time of the year. This is an ideal cake to give as a gift because it keeps really well for at least two months if carefully wrapped in foil.

Preheat oven to 180°C (350°F). Line a 20 cm (8″) tin with non-stick baking paper.

flour, plain	*⅔ cup*	Sieve all into a large bowl.
cocoa powder	*2 tablespoons*	
cinnamon	*½ teaspoon*	
cloves, ground	*¼ teaspoon*	
nutmeg, ground	*¼ teaspoon*	
coriander, ground	*¼ teaspoon*	
hazelnuts, roasted	*125 g (4 oz)*	Add to above.
almonds, roasted	*125 g (4 oz)*	
glacé apricots, chopped	*30 g (1 oz)*	
glacé cherries	*30 g (1 oz)*	
crystallised ginger	*60 g (2 oz)*	
mixed peel	*60 g (2 oz)*	
dark chocolate, grated	*60 g (2 oz)*	Melt. Keep warm (see p.9).
sugar, white	*⅓ cup*	Stir slowly over a very low heat in the smallest pan you have. Cook, without stirring, for about four minutes until a little dropped in a cup of cold water forms a soft ball. *Don't overcook.* Quickly mix together the syrup and chocolate. Add this mixture to the flour and fruit and mix well. Spoon into the tin and smooth gently. Bake for 35 minutes. Leave to cool in the tin. Dust the top with icing sugar to absorb any stickiness.
butter	*2 tablespoons*	
clear honey	*½ cup*	

STAINED GLASS CHRISTMAS CAKE

I do not know if this is a traditional Australian Christmas cake but I had never come across it until I came to Australia over 20 years ago. This is my version. Slice it thinly as it is very rich. This cake keeps well if it's wrapped in non-stick foil and refrigerated. The fruit shouldn't be chopped finely as the eye-appeal of this cake is in the large pieces of fruit and nuts when the cake is sliced.

Preheat oven to 150°C (300°F). Line a 23 cm × 13 cm (9″ × 5″) tin with non-stick baking paper.

glacé cherries	*1 cup*	Mix all in a large bowl.
glacé apricots, chopped	*¾ cup*	
glacé pineapple, chopped	*¾ cup*	
glacé ginger	*¾ cup*	
Brazil nuts, whole	*1 cup*	
whole pecans	*1½ cups*	
plain flour	*¾ cup*	Sieve and mix with the fruit and nuts.
baking powder	*½ teaspoon*	
mixed spice	*1 teaspoon*	
cardamom, ground	*1 teaspoon*	
castor sugar	*½ cup*	Beat together very well. Mix gently with all the other ingredients. Spoon into the tin. Level the top gently. Bake for 1½–2 hours or until firm. Cool in the tin. Wrap in foil until ready to decorate.
brandy	*2 tablespoons*	
vanilla essence	*1 teaspoon*	
eggs, beaten	*3*	
To decorate:		
jelly marmalade	*¼ cup*	Warm and brush over the cake.
assorted glacé fruit and nuts		Arrange decoratively over the top of the cake. Brush with the remaining marmalade.

CHRISTMAS CAKE

This cake is very easy to make being of the boiled-fruit variety. It keeps well and is delicious and moist.

Pre-set oven to 160°C (325°F). Line a 23 cm (9″) round or a 20 cm (8″) square tin with two layers of non-stick baking paper, coming 5 cm (2″) above the top of the tin.

mixed dried fruit	*1 kg (2 lb)*	Combine in a saucepan. Stir over
sugar, dark brown	*1 cup*	a low heat until the butter is
butter	*250 g (½ lb)*	melted and the sugar dissolved.
glacé pineapple, chopped	*60 g (2 oz)*	Bring to a boil and simmer,
glacé apricots, chopped	*60 g (2 oz)*	covered, for 5 minutes. Allow to
almonds, slivered	*½ cup*	go completely cold.
brandy	*½ cup*	
orange juice, fresh	*¼ cup*	
lemon juice, fresh	*¼ cup*	
black treacle	*1 tablespoon*	Mix well together. Stir into above.
grated orange zest (p.14)	*2 teaspoons*	
eggs, beaten	*5*	
plain flour	*1¾ cups*	Sift twice. Stir very gently into
self-raising flour	*⅓ cup*	above. Spread in the tin. Bake for
cardamom, ground	*½ teaspoon*	2–2½ hours. Cover the cooked
soda bicarbonate	*½ teaspoon*	cake with baking paper and
mixed spice	*½ teaspoon*	allow to go completely cold in the
		tin.

MAZURKA CAKE

Here is another Christmas cake—this time from Russia. It is baked in quite a thin layer, more like a slab cake. I like this cake very much as it is possible to cut smaller pieces than a conventional cake. It will store for about one month if well wrapped and refrigerated.

Preheat oven to 150°C (300°F). Grease a swiss-roll tin and line with non-stick baking paper.

glacé cherries	*60 g (2 oz)*	Mix well in a large bowl.
glacé apricots, chopped	*60 g (2 oz)*	
glacé pineapple, chopped	*60 g (2 oz)*	
mixed peel	*60 g (2 oz)*	
currants	*125 g (4 oz)*	
sultanas	*125 g (4 oz)*	
seedless raisins	*125 g (4 oz)*	
dates, chopped	*125 g (4 oz)*	
apricots, dried, chopped	*125 g (4 oz)*	
almonds, blanched, chopped	*125 g (4 oz)*	
eggs, beaten	*3*	Mix together and add to above,
honey, thin	*⅓ cup*	blending well.
plain flour	*1¼ cups*	Add. Mix thoroughly. Spread in the tin. Smooth down. Cook for about one hour or until firm in the centre. Cool in the tin.

DATE AND WALNUT LOAF

This moist, tasty loaf is only at its best for about one week but has the advantage of freezing well. Dried walnuts can sometimes be very bitter (see p.11 for a note on de-bittering).

Preheat oven to 180°C (350°F). Grease and flour 2 small loaf tins.

boiling water	2 cups	Stir gently over a low heat until the sugar and butter are melted. Bring to boil. Remove from the heat and allow to go completely cold.
mixed spice	2 teaspoons	
butter	4 tablespoons	
dates, coarsely chopped	500 g (1 lb)	
soda bicarbonate	2 teaspoons	
sugar, dark brown	1½ cups	
vanilla essence	2 teaspoons	Mix into above.
egg, beaten	2	
self-raising flour, sifted	3½ cups	Mix gently but thoroughly with the above. Bake for ¾–1 hour. Cover the top with non-stick baking paper and allow to cool in the tin.
walnuts, chopped	3 cups	

CHOCOLATE CHIP BROWNIES

These brownies should be made a day or two before you give them away as they do not keep well for more than a week. They are the perfect gift for a 'chocolaholic'.

It's difficult to tell you how long to cook brownies as the usual skewer test doesn't work. If you insert the skewer it should come out damp with mixture clinging to it but not be soggy.

Preheat oven to 180°C (350°F). Grease a 20 cm (8″) square pan or a rectangular pan which has the same overall dimensions.

dark chocolate	60 g (2 oz)	Melt gently together.
butter	100 g (3½ oz)	
vanilla essence	2 teaspoons	Mix with above.
eggs, beaten	2	
sugar, white	1 cup	Sift together. Fold into above.
plain flour	½ cup	
baking powder	½ teaspoon	
pecans, chopped	½ cup	Add. Mix gently. Pour into the pan. Bake for 30–40 minutes. Ice and mark into squares while still warm. Cool in the tin.
chocolate chips	1 cup	
sultanas	½ cup	
Icing:		
dark chocolate, melted	90 g (3 oz)	Mix together and spread over the still warm brownies.
yoghurt	1 tablespoon	

TINY CHRISTMAS CAKES

It's possible to make a delightful gift basket containing Christmas tea or dinner for one or two people. These little cakes are just the right size and are fruity without being too rich. These cakes don't store for as long as a large cake but if wrapped in foil and stored in airtight containers will keep for about two weeks.

Preheat oven to 160°C (325°F). Grease 12 deep muffin tins.

mixed fruit	1 cup	Combine in a large bowl. Cover and leave for 12 hours. Stir occasionally.
glacé cherries, chopped	⅓ cup	
glacé pineapple, chopped	⅓ cup	
glacé apricots, chopped	⅓ cup	
walnuts, chopped	¼ cup	
almonds, blanched, chopped	¼ cup	
brandy	3 tablespoons	
vanilla essence	1 teaspoon	
sugar, light brown	¾ cup	Cream together until very pale.
butter	125 g (4 oz)	
eggs, medium, beaten	2	Add slowly to the butter mixture, beating continuously.
plain flour	1 cup	Sift together twice. Fold into the butter mixture and then into the fruit. Mix gently but thoroughly. Divide the mixture between the muffin tins. Smooth the tops. Bake for about 45 minutes or until cooked. Cool in the tins.
self-raising flour	¼ cup	
ginger, ground	¼ teaspoon	
nutmeg, ground	¼ teaspoon	
cinnamon, ground	1 teaspoon	
salt	⅛ teaspoon	
cardamom, ground	¼ teaspoon	

Decorate with blanched almonds and glacé cherries split in half. Alternatively the cakes may be iced when they are cold or glazed with warm, sieved apricot jam.

PIKELETS

Pikelet mixes make a good gift for a busy person who likes to offer homemade food but doesn't have much time for preparation. I keep a variety of pikelet mixes in my store cupboard, some are delicate for afternoon tea, some are more solid for satisfying hungry gardeners. These mixes are useful for taking on camping holidays as they are light to carry, don't 'go off', and need little preparation. The pikelets may be eaten plain but are yummy with butter, maple syrup, golden syrup, honey or any topping you like. The instructions for making the pikelets should be included with the gift.

To make up a batch of pikelets from the following two recipes:

pikelet mix	1 cup	Beat all together to a thick cream. Drop tablespoonfuls on a preheated, lightly greased frypan. Cook over moderate heat until bubbles appear and burst. Turn and cook the other side. Keep warm in a tea-towel until all are cooked.
egg	1	
yoghurt	1 tablespoon	
milk or water	½–1 cup	

CAMPERS' PIKELET MIX

The addition of dried milk in this recipe makes it possible to add only water to make the pikelets. These are very filling and give you energy.

self-raising flour	3 cups	Sift together.
wholemeal self-raising flour	2 cups	
baking powder	1 teaspoon	
quick rolled oats	1 cup	Mix with above.
sultanas	1 cup	
currants	1 cup	
sunflower seeds	½ cup	
skimmed milk powder	2 cups	
sugar	4 tablespoons	
sesame seeds, roasted, ground	3 tablespoons	
almonds, roasted, chopped	1 cup	

CITRUS PIKELET MIX

Delicious, light citrus-flavoured pikelets. The method for making citrus powder will be found on p.69.

self-raising flour	8 cups	Sift together twice.
soda bicarbonate	2 teaspoons	

sugar, white	*1 cup*	Mix all together.
sultanas, chopped	*½ cup*	
sunflower seeds, toasted	*½ cup*	
citrus powder (see p.69)	*3 tablespoons*	

GOLDEN GRANOLA

When I lived in a commune we devised many different muesli and granola mixes. These were the staple food on which to do a good morning's work. I have included my latest recipe because, like the pikelets, it looks good, tastes good, and makes a great gift for people who like to eat well but live very busy lives. My breakfast each morning is a small bowl of granola with a piece of fruit chopped into it, yoghurt and skimmed milk. This meals lasts my body for about five hours. The cooking of this cereal is most important. You will need to stay close to the stove to turn the mixture *very* often—as the colour begins to change the stirring will need to be done as much as every 30 seconds until the mixture is a deep golden nut brown and no longer sticky.

Don't use quick-cooking rolled oats for this recipe, as they don't crisp. Buy the quite thick-looking rolled oats from the health food store. With the help of my husband I cook a *huge* quantity of this granola, package it in large bags, and store it in my freezer.

Preheat oven to 220°C (430°F). Large roasting pans are needed.

raw, hulled buckwheat	*2 cups*	Mix together in a large bowl.
rolled oats (*not quick*)	*5 cups*	
oat bran	*2 cups*	
desiccated coconut	*1 cup*	
sunflower seeds	*½ cup*	
peanuts, chopped	*1 cup*	
almonds, chopped	*1 cup*	
honey	*1 cup*	Melt together. Pour over the mixture. Mix really well. Divide between large roasting pans. Stir often during the cooking as the mixture will burn very easily. When the granola is a rich golden brown and no longer sticky— about 20–30 minutes—take from the oven and spread on a clean working surface to cool.
safflower oil	*½ cup*	
peanut butter	*½ cup*	
dried apricots	*½ cup*	Chop all (except the sultanas) quite finely. Mix into the cooled granola. Mix well and package.
pitted prunes	*½ cup*	
dried dates	*½ cup*	
sultanas	*½ cup*	

BISCUITS

How do they taste?
They taste like more.

—H.L. Mencken (1880–1956)

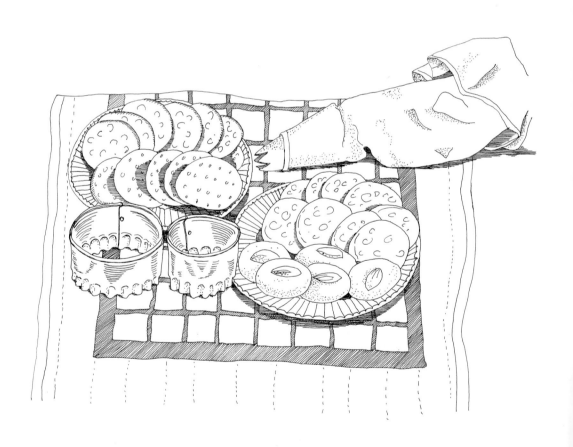

Biscuits are always a good gift especially during holiday times when there are likely to be friends calling in for a drink or a cup of tea. Most biscuits keep well if stored in airtight tins or jars.

HAZELNUT BISCUITS

Preheat oven to 180°C (350°F). Grease and flour baking tray. Roast and skin the hazelnuts (see p.11).

plain flour	185 g (6 oz)	Sift together twice.
castor sugar	60 g (2 oz)	
cinnamon	1 teaspoon	
butter, softened	125 g (¼ lb)	Rub in.
egg, beaten	1 whole	Add. Mix well and shape into a ball. Roll out to 0.5 cm (¼") thick. Cut into shapes.
egg yolk	1	Brush over the biscuits.
hazelnuts, chopped	60 g	Mix together, sprinkle over biscuits and press gently. Bake for 15–20 minutes. Cool on trays.
icing sugar	1 tablespoon	

ALMOND SHORTBREAD

Shortbread is always an acceptable gift. It may be shaped into two rounds 1 cm (½") thick or shaped with the edges crimped or pressed into a baking tray and marked into fingers before cooking. It's possible to buy beautiful shortbread moulds which give a professional appearance to the finished biscuits.

Preheat oven to 170°C (340°F). Grease oven trays.

castor sugar	½ cup	Sift together several times.
plain flour	2 cups	
cornflour	1 cup	
butter	250 g (½ lb)	Rub into above until the mixture begins to cling together. Knead very lightly. Form into a ball and shape as suggested in the introduction to this recipe. Prick the dough all over with a fork before baking. Cook for about 20 minutes or until golden brown. Leave to cool. Pack in airtight containers.
almond essence	1 teaspoon	

SHORTBREAD

To shape, see the preliminary instructions for almond shortbread.

Preheat oven to 160°C (325°F).

plain flour	*2 cups*	Sift together several times.
rice flour	*2 tablespoons*	
icing sugar	*⅓ cup*	
butter, chopped	*250 g (½ lb)*	Rub into the above mix using fingertips. Mix and knead gently until ball is formed. Shape and bake.

CITRUS BISCUITS

Preheat oven to 200°C (400°F). Grease oven trays.

butter	*100 g (3½ oz)*	Melt, don't overheat.
castor sugar	*100 g (3½ oz)*	Add all to the melted butter.
egg yolks, beaten	*2*	
orange zest (see p.14)	*2 oranges*	
plain flour	*150 g (6 oz)*	Sift together twice. Mix with the above to a smooth biscuit dough. Add a little beaten egg white if the mixture feels too dry or crumbly. Wrap and chill for a short time until firm. Roll out to 4 mm (⅛″) thick. Cut into circles or rings. Bake for 10 minutes. Cool on trays. Ice.
baking powder	*1 teaspoon*	
cornflour	*100 g (3½ oz)*	
Icing:		
icing sugar, sieved	*125 g (5 oz)*	Mix and spread over biscuits.
orange juice	*1 tablespoon*	
lemon juice	*1 tablespoon*	
almonds, blanched	*½ cup*	Chop finely. Sprinkle over the iced biscuits before the icing sets.

APRICOT RINGS

Preheat oven to 180°C (300°F). Grease baking trays.

butter, softened	*½ cup*	Beat together until pale.
sugar, white	*¾ cup*	

eggs, beaten milk	2 4 tablespoons	Add slowly while beating well to prevent curdling.
plain flour salt baking powder	3 cups pinch 1 teaspoon	Sift together twice. Mix into above to form dough. Knead gently. Roll on a floured boards to 3 mm (⅛") thick. Cut into rounds. Cut centres out of half the rounds using a smaller cutter. Cook for 10–15 minutes till pale golden brown. Cool on the trays. Store in airtight containers.
apricot jam, sieved icing sugar, sieved	½ cup	Before giving as a gift, sandwich the biscuits together with the jam and dust with icing sugar.

LEBKUCHEN

Spice biscuits which, in Germany where they originate, are cut into festive shapes for hanging on the Christmas tree.

Preheat oven to 160°C (325°F). Grease and flour baking trays.

plain flour baking powder cinnamon, ground ginger, ground nutmeg, ground coriander, ground	2 cups 2 teaspoons 1 teaspoon 1 teaspoon ½ teaspoon ¼ teaspoon	Sift together twice.
almonds, ground hazelnuts, ground apricots, dried, finely chopped	2 tablespoons 2 tablespoons 1 tablespoon	Add to the above mixture and make a well in the centre.
clear honey sugar oil	¾ cup 2½ tablespoons 2 tablespoons	Melt together.
cocoa powder egg yolk, beaten lemon juice	1 teaspoon 1 ½ teaspoon	Add to the honey. Mix. Pour into the flour well. Mix until a firm dough is formed. Wrap in plastic and rest for one hour out of the refrigerator. Knead lightly on a floured surface. Roll to 0.5 cm (⅕") thick. Cut into shapes. Bake for 12–15 minutes to a golden brown. Cool on a rack. Allow to go completely cold.
dark chocolate	185 g (6 oz)	Melt (see p.9). Spread over the base of the cold biscuits.

KIPPFERL

A most delicious, light, crisp Austrian biscuit. The recipe was given to me by my German daughter-in-law and it is now one of our favourites. Buy the ground almonds rather than grinding your own as the home-prepared ones seem oiler. If the weather is very hot you will need to form the Kippferls in small amounts, leaving the remaining dough in the refrigerator until you are ready to form more.

Preheat oven to 170°C (340°F). Grease baking trays.

butter castor sugar vanilla essence	250 g (½ lb) ¾ cup 1 teaspoon	Beat together until very pale and fluffy.
ground almonds plain flour salt	1½ cups up to 2½ cups pinch	Mix in well. Use enough flour to make a firm dough.
		Wrap in plastic wrap and chill for one to two hours. Roll into walnut-sized balls and then form into crescents. Chill in the refrigerator for 10 minutes. Bake for 15–20 minutes until golden brown. Cool for a few minutes. Dust with sieved icing sugar. Allow to cool before storing.

MACAROONS

Preheat oven to 180°C (350°F). Grease baking trays or line with rice paper.

ground almonds castor sugar	2½ cups 1 cup	Mix together.
egg white, beaten kirsch almond essence	2 2 teaspoons 4 drops	Add. Mix until a ball is formed. Shape into walnut-sized balls. Place well apart on the baking trays.
almonds, split, blanched		Moisten each ½ almond and press gently into the macaroon to flatten the tops a little. Bake for 20 minutes. Cool on racks.

CRISP BUTTER BISCUITS

)0°F). Line baking trays with non-stick baking paper.

½ cup ½ cup	Cream together until pale and fluffy.
3	Add slowly, beating well.
½ lemon	Add, beating well.
1½ cups	Add a little at a time until a fairly firm but not dry dough is formed. Wrap in plastic and refrigerate until firm (for no longer than 30 minutes). Take pieces the size of a large walnut, roll into a rope, place on the trays and form into 'S' shapes. Flatten slightly.
1	Brush with the egg white. Sprinkle with the sugar and bake for 10–15 minutes till lightly browned and set. Cool on a rack.

RICCIARELLI

most a confection. They make a good gift for anyone. The ground
quality and very finely ground.

2 cups ¾ cup	Pound together with a pestle and mortar or something similar until well blended.
¾ cup 4 drops ½ teaspoon	Mix with above.
2	Beat till frothy. Mix to a stiff paste, adding more icing sugar if needed. Take small pieces and form into shapes like large almonds. Place on a wire rack and dry for 24 hours. Place on greased baking tray or line trays with rice paper. Bake at 120°C (250°F) for 30–40 minutes. Dust with icing sugar. Cool. Dust again with icing sugar. Store in airtight containers.

CHOCOLATE-DIPPED BUTTER BISCUITS

Preheat oven to 180°C (350°F). Lightly grease and flour baking sheets.

butter, softened castor sugar	*1 cup* *¼ cup*	Beat together until pale and fluffy.
vanilla essence	*½ teaspoon*	Add and beat.
plain flour	*2 cups*	Stir in gently. Spoon into a piping bag with a star nozzle. Pipe into 5 cm (2″) lengths onto the trays. Bake for 12–15 minutes until pale golden brown. Leave to cool for a few minutes on the trays. Finish cooling on wire cake racks.
compound chocolate, melted	*125 g (4 oz)*	Spread on the underside of the biscuits. Allow to set.
icing sugar, sieved		Sprinkle on the biscuits before giving as a gift.

CHEESE STRAWS

Preheat oven to 190°C (375°F). Grease baking trays.

butter plain flour	*¼ cup* *1¼ cups*	Rub together with the fingertips until the mixture looks like fine breadcrumbs.
cheddar cheese, grated cayenne salt & black pepper	*1 cup* *pinch* *pinch*	Add. Mix well.
egg yolk, beaten lemon juice water, if needed	*1* *1 tablespoon*	Add. Mix to a firm dough. Add water if needed. Roll between non-stick baking paper to 0.5 cm (¼″) thick. Cut into 15 cm × 0.5 cm (6″ × ¼″) strips. Roll out any scraps. Cut a few circles with a fluted scone-cutter and cut the centres from these with a slightly smaller cutter to form rings. Bake for 10–12 minutes or until golden brown. Cool. Thread straws into the rings before packing into boxes.

CHEESY WATER-BISCUITS

Preheat oven to 230°C (450°F). Grease baking trays.

butter plain flour	30 g (1 oz) 1 cup	Rub together with the fingertips until the mixture resembles breadcrumbes.
cheddar, finely grated salt mustard powder cracked black pepper	2 tablespoons ⅛ teaspoon ⅛ teaspoon ⅛ teaspoon	Add.
lemon juice water	1 tablespoon	Add. Mix to a firm but not dry dough ball. Add more water to achieve this if necessary. Don't knead. Roll out very thinly. Cut to shapes. Prick well with a fork. Place on baking sheet.
egg yolk, beaten water	1 1 tablespoon	Mix together. Brush crackers lightly. Bake till crisp, golden and bubbly.

CRACKED-PEPPER CRACKERS

Preheat oven to 180°C (350°F). Grease baking trays.

butter skimmed milk	30 g ½ cup	Warm together until butter has melted. Don't overheat.
plain flour cayenne pepper salt dried mixed herbs	1½ cups pinch ¼ teaspoon ½ teaspoon	Add and mix to a stiff paste. Place on a board and beat with a rolling pin until smooth. Roll out very thinly to a rough rectangle. Cover with a clean cloth and let rest for 30 minutes. Cut into rounds larger than you want as these biscuits will shrink while cooking. Prick well with a fork. Arrange on baking trays.
milk cracked pepper		Brush the tops with milk and sprinkle with cracked green or black pepper. Press lightly. Bake for 6–10 minutes until a good golden brown. Cool on the trays. Store in airtight containers.

SESAME CHEESE BISCUITS

These biscuits keep well for about one week only, but if they are being given as a part of a cheese and biscuit basket they will be eaten quite quickly. A bought package pastry is used, so these biscuits are both easy and speedy to make.

Preheat oven to 180°C (350°F). Grease oven trays.

short pastry mix	*250 g (½ lb)*	Mix all together. Add enough
salt	*½ teaspoon*	water to make a soft, but not wet,
dry mustard	*¼ teaspoon*	dough. Knead lightly. Roll out
cheddar, grated	*½ cup*	thinly. Brush with milk. Cut into
water	*about ⅓ cup*	circles or squares.
sesame seeds		Sprinkle over quite thickly, press in gently. Bake for 15 minutes or until the biscuits are golden brown. Cool on trays. Store in airtight containers.

DESSERTS & CANDYING

Cooking is like love.
It should be entered into with abandon or not at all.
—Harriet Van Horne (b.1920)

Desserts

The following recipes for fruits marinated in various alcohols are absolutely wonderful, rich and intensely flavoured. The fruits may be drained and served with a toothpick stuck in each one as an after-dinner treat with a glass of liqueur, or served in *small* dishes with their juice and topped with cream or ice-cream, as a dessert. Whichever way you serve them remember that small quantities are sufficient.

CUMQUATS IN BRANDY

For those of you fortunate enough to have a cumquat tree here is a delicious and unusual dessert or after-dinner treat.

cumquats	500 g (1 lb)	Pierce all over with a needle.
sugar, white	2 cups	Layer with the fruit in a wide-mouthed jar.
brandy	3 cups (approx)	Pour over to completely cover the fruit. Seal and leave in a cool, dark place to mature for 3–4 months. Invert the jar occasionally.

BRANDIED PRUNES

prunes, pitted sugar, dark brown strong, fresh tea	500 g (1 lb) ½ cup 2 cups	Simmer for 10 minutes. Cool. Drain.
cinnamon sticks lemon peel (no white) orange peel (no white) crystallised ginger	2 4 strips 2 strips 12 pieces	Arrange decoratively in a wide-mouthed jar with the prunes. Quarter-fill the jar with the reserved liquid.
brandy	to cover	Fill the jar and seal tightly. Leave to mature for at least 2 weeks before using.

MIDDLE EASTERN FRUIT SALAD

This dessert is exotic and rich. It will keep well in the refrigerator for about four weeks. Serve small portions in glass dishes, pipe with cream, and sprinkle a few roast pine nuts or roast slivered almonds over the cream.

glacé cherries	60 g (2 oz)	Soak all together in a wide-mouthed jar. Top up with apple juice as needed. Invert the jar every day to dissolve the sugar. Leave for one week before using.
dried apricots	125 g (4 oz)	
glacé pineapple	90 g (3 oz)	
dates, stoned	90 g (3 oz)	
sultanas	30 g (1 oz)	
raisins, stoned	30 g (1 oz)	
sugar, white	¼ cup	
brandy	½ cup	
rosewater (see p.13)	¼ cup	
apple juice	to cover	

SHERRIED APRICOTS AND PEACHES

water	1½ cups	Bring slowly to a boil, stirring
sugar	1 cup	gently to dissolve the sugar.
lemon peel, no pith	1 lemon	Simmer for 5 minutes.
dried apricots	250 g (½ lb)	Add. Cover and simmer for 10
dried peaches	250 g (½ lb)	minutes. Leave for 12 hours. Drain. Reserve syrup.
sweet sherry	1 cup (approx)	Add to the syrup.
crystallised ginger	¾ cup	Layer with the fruit in a wide-mouthed jar. Pour the syrup over, adding more sherry if needed. The fruit must be covered by about 2.5 cm (1″) of liquid. Seal and leave for 2 weeks before using.

ORANGES IN COINTREAU

It's important to use thin-skinned oranges for this recipe, as the thick-skinned variety would make the finished product very bitter.

thin-skinned oranges	8	Discard ends which have no flesh. Slice thinly and remove pips.
sugar, white	4 cups	Layer with the orange slices. Cover and leave for 24 hours.
water	½ cup	Simmer gently together for 5
cloves	8	minutes. Add the sugar and
cinnamon stick, broken	7.5 cm (3″)	oranges and poach very gently until the peel is tender and transparent. Add more water if the syrup is getting too thick.
sweet white wine	¼ cup	Add. Mix gently. Lift oranges
Cointreau	¼ cup	carefully into wide-mouthed jars, overlapping the slices ornamentally. Leave 4 cm (1½″) headspace. Fill the jars with the syrup, adding more wine if needed.

FIGS IN PORT

water	1½ cups	Bring to boil slowly, stirring
sugar, brown	1 cup	gently to dissolve sugar. Simmer
cinnamon stick, broken	1	for 5 minutes.
cloves	4	
dried whole figs	500 g (1 lb)	Add. Cover and simmer for 20 minutes. Leave for 24 hours. Drain. Reserve the syrup. Put the fruit into a wide-mouthed jar.
brandy	2 tablespoons	Add to the syrup, pour over the
port	½–1 cup	figs. Top up with extra port if needed, to cover the figs by 2.5 cm (1"). Mature in a cool, dark place for 6 weeks before using.

Candying

GLACÉ FIGS

Glacé figs make a lovely gift particularly if the figs were grown as well as prepared by you. When I lived on a farm we had rainwater tanks which were perfect places for drying fruit of all kinds during our long hot summers. The muslin-covered wire-mesh trays were brought in at night to protect the fruit from dew and marauding possums. The glacé figs may be dried out of doors if you live in a climate which has several consecutive days of clear hot sunshine. To dry figs in the oven you will need to set your temperature as low as it will go. Put the figs well separated on racks low in the oven. Leave the door slightly ajar and rotate the racks often.

firm figs	2 kg (4 lb)	Pierce all over with a darning needle.
water	3 cups	Stir over a low heat until the
white sugar	6 cups	sugar is dissolved. Bring to a boil.
lemon peel, no pith	2 lemons	Add the figs. Simmer for 45 minutes. Drain and cool. Repeat process twice more. See opening remarks for drying process. The figs should take 3–6 hours to dry, depending on the temperature of the oven. Roll in sieved icing sugar before packing.

CANDIED PEEL

The flavour of homemade candied peel is intense and the perfume is richly aromatic. Once you have made and experienced your own product you will never again buy candied peel, particularly as this is the part of the fruit usually thrown away so it has cost you nothing. If liked the peel may be cut into small pieces instead of leaving it in quarters.

oranges/lemons or mixture	6	Cut a little from both ends of the fruit. Slice into quarters lengthwise through the peel and pith and ease away from the flesh. Put in a basin.
soda bicarbonate water, hot	2 teaspoons 1 cup	Dissolve together. Pour over the rind and top up with boiling water to cover completely. Stand for 2 hours. Drain. Put in a saucepan, cover with cold water and simmer till perfectly tender. Drain and put back into the bowl.
sugar, white water	2 cups 2 cups	Put into the pan, stir over a low heat until dissolved. Pour over the peel. Stand in a covered bowl for 2 days. Strain the syrup into the pan.
sugar, white	1 cup	Add to syrup. Stir over a low heat until the sugar is dissolved. Add peel and simmer until transparent. Drain. Dry the peel on racks in the lowest part of the oven with the temperature as low as it will go and the door slightly open. Simmer the syrup for 20 minutes, take off the heat and dip the dried peel into the syrup. Drain and dry as before. Allow to cool, and store in airtight containers.

GRAPEFRUIT CANDY

In medieval days the candied peel of citrus fruits was the main sweetmeat. The texture of this candied peel when first made is similar to a 'jube' but it dries out with time to a more sugary texture.

grapefruit	*3*	Trim the ends and slice lengthwise through the peel and pith into quarters; ease away from the flesh. Cut the quarters into strips and cut each strip in half. Put in a bowl.
soda bicarbonate water, hot	*2 teaspoons* *1 cup*	Dissolve together, pour over the peel. Cover with boiling water. Leave for one hour. Drain and put in a pan. Cover with cold water. Bring to a boil and immediately drain. Cover with more cold water and repeat the process 6 times. The final time the peel should be simmered until soft. Drain.
white sugar water	*3 cups* *2 cups*	Stir over a low heat until the sugar is dissolved. Add the grapefruit slices. Cook gently until the peel is transparent. Drain on cake racks, keeping each piece separate. Cover with cheesecloth and leave for 2–3 days to become dry on the outside. Toss in icing sugar. Leave for a few hours. Toss again. Store in airtight containers.

CRYSTALLISED FLOWERS

A box of petals would be a terrific gift for an ardent cook. The best flowers to crystallise are violets and borage; the best petals are carnation and rose. The latter needs to have the white pithy piece at the base of the leaves removed as this is quite bitter.

Beat an egg white until it's broken down but not too frothy. Using a very fine paintbrush, coat each petal with a *thin* layer of egg white. Sprinkle with castor sugar making sure that every part of the petal is covered. Place on a fine rack or fine mesh, cover with greaseproof paper and leave to dry in a warm room. Store in single layers separated by greaseproof paper in airtight containers.

CANDIED APRICOTS

To store the apricots it is necessary to layer them with non-stick baking paper between each layer.

sugar, white	1 cup	Combine all in a small pan. Stir over a low heat until the sugar is dissolved. Bring to a boil and without stirring, cook to a 'soft ball' stage (see p.11) for about 5–7 minutes.
lemon zest (see p.14)	½ teaspoon	
orange zest	1 teaspoon	
cardamom, ground	¼ teaspoon	
cinnamon, ground	⅛ teaspoon	
water	¾ cup	
dried apricots	185 g (6 oz)	Add. Turn heat as low as possible. Cook for 8 minutes, stirring often. Place the fruit, not touching each other, on racks to drain. When cool, roll in icing sugar.

SWEETS & CHOCOLATES

We never repent of having eaten too little.
—Thomas Jefferson (1743–1826)

There is no better gift than that of chocolates or sweets. Most of these are very simple to make and with a little care can taste and look as good, if not better, than the bought variety (p.9 has instructions for the handling of chocolate).

The first recipes in this section are for truffles and balls. These may be covered with any of the following: plain or toasted coconut, cocoa powder, grated chocolate, very finely chopped nuts or melted compound chocolate—choose whichever seems to suit the recipe.

BRANDY BALLS

These are rich and delicious. They keep very well but if the weather is hot they should be refrigerated. See p.11 for preparation of hazelnuts and p.9 for chocolate topping.

chocolate sponge cake	*250 g (8 oz)*	Crumble the cake finely. Mix all well together.
icing sugar, sieved	*1 cup, lightly packed*	
hazelnuts, roasted, ground	*1 cup*	
cocoa	*½ cup*	
brandy	*½ cup (approx.)*	Add sufficient to make a firm texture. Roll into small balls. Refrigerate until firm then dip in melted chocolate.

APRICOT NUT TRUFFLES

dried apricots, finely chopped	*60 g (2 oz)*	Mix together. Cover and leave overnight.
Cointreau	*2 tablespoons*	
dark chocolate	*250 g (½ lb)*	Melt (see p.9).
cashews, roasted, finely chopped	*½ cup*	Mix with all above. Refrigerate for about 10 minutes or until stiff enough to mould.
compound chocolate	*155 g (5 oz)*	Melt together. Dip truffles. Allow to set on waxed paper in the refrigerator. Drizzle decoratively with chocolate if liked.
white vegetable shortening	*4 teaspoons*	

RUM BALLS

dark chocolate	*125 g (4 oz)*	Melt (see p.9).
dark rum	*2 tablespoons*	Add. Stir until butter is melted and mixed in.
butter, softened	*60 g (2 oz)*	
sifted icing sugar	*⅓ cup*	Add.
ground almonds	*¾ cup (approx.)*	Mix in enough to make a dough. Rest in the refrigerator until firm enough to handle. Roll into small balls. See the beginning of this section for finishing.

HAZELNUT TRUFFLES

These easy and delicious truffles may be decorated with drizzles of white or milk chocolate to contrast with the coating.

hazelnut chocolate spread	*1 jar*	Warm a little to soften
rum	*1 tablespoon*	Add. Mix well.
hazelnuts, roasted, ground	*1¼ cups approx*	Mix with the spread. Cool until the mixture is firm enough to form into balls.
compound chocolate	*280 g (9 oz)*	Melt (see p.9). Dip the balls, put on waxed paper in the refrigerator to harden.

HAZELNUT CREAMS

compound chocolate	*250 g (8 oz)*	Melt (see p.9).
condensed milk	*½ a 400 g (13 oz) can*	Add. Stir.
brandy	*1 tablespoon*	
hazelnuts, roasted, ground	*90 g (3 oz)*	Add enough to form a 'pipable' texture. Pipe into foil chocolate cases. Top with either ½ a roasted hazelnut or half a glacé cherry.

CREAM TRUFFLES

These truffles are made with cream which is boiled to improve the keeping qualities but even so these are best eaten within 10 days.

cream	*1 cup*	Bring to a boil in a small pan.
dark chocolate	*300 g (9½ oz)*	Add. Stir till melted.
cashew nuts, roasted, chopped	*¼ cup*	Chop finely. Add and mix.
dried pineapple, chopped	*½ cup*	
sultanas, chopped	*¼ cup*	
brandy	*3 tablespoons*	Add. Mix well. Leave to firm. Roll into balls and either roll in one of the coatings suggested at the beginning of this section or leave plain.

DATE AND GINGER FINGERS

crystallised ginger dates, finely chopped	6 tablespoons 1 cup	Mince finely. Measure after mincing. Shape into fingers 1 cm × 5 cm (½" × 2").
compound chocolate	220 g (7 oz)	Melt (see p.9). Dip fingers. Place on waxed paper to set.

KARTOFFELN

These yummy little morsels are good to make at Christmas time when marzipan is available. The marzipan needs to be of the old fashioned, real variety—the new soft type doesn't work, unless you add a lot of icing sugar. If you can't buy the correct paste, you can make your own (see below). These balls keep well but need to be refrigerated.

instant coffee powder coffee liqueur	1 teaspoon 2 tablespoons	Mix together.
marzipan, softened	200 g (6½ oz)	Knead with the liquid until well blended. Form into small balls, dipping your hands into warm water occasionally to prevent the mixture sticking.
icing sugar cocoa powder	¾ cup 2 teaspoons	Sift together. Roll balls in the mixture. Refrigerate.

MARZIPAN (ALMOND PASTE)

This recipe is for an uncooked marzipan which I find almost as good as the cooked variety and very much quicker and simpler to make. It may be used to cover cakes or coloured, flavoured and shaped to make sweets or cake decorations. Marzipan may also be flavoured and dipped into melted compound chocolate.

icing sugar, sifted almonds, ground	2 cups 2 cups	Mix together.
almond essence	1 teaspoon	Add.
egg yolks, beaten	2	Add enough to form a stiff dough. If too wet add more ground almonds. If too dry add a little lemon juice. Turn onto a board dusted with icing sugar and knead until smooth.

APRICOT SLICES

These slices are particularly good for children. They satisfy a sweet tooth but contain so much nutrition that there are none of the disadvantages of conventional sweets. At Easter time I shape the mixture into little eggs to give to my grandchildren.

dried apricots, chopped	½ cup	Simmer together for 10 minutes. Leave for 2 hours to cool.
orange juice, fresh	¼ cup	
almonds, ground	¼ cup	Mix to a firm dough. Roll into a log (see p.10). Roll in extra toasted coconut. Refrigerate until very firm. Cut in slices about 5 cm (¼") thick. Store in an airtight container.
nuts, roasted, chopped	¼ cup	
sesame seeds, crushed	1 tablespoon	
currants, chopped	¼ cup	
prunes, chopped	¼ cup	
dried milk	¼ cup	
coconut, toasted, desiccated	¼ cup	

APRICOT JELLIES

Very more-ish little morsels. The soft type of dried apricots are the best to use.

dried apricots	250 g (½ lb)	Blend until a soft paste is formed.
orange zest	½ teaspoon	
Cointreau or brandy	2 tablespoons	
icing sugar	½ cup	Add slowly until a stiffish paste is formed. The mixture should not be sloppy but more liqueur may be added it it's too dry. Roll into 1 cm (½") balls and then in icing sugar. Leave to dry for 24 hours before putting in individual paper cases and packing in airtight boxes.

FROSTED DATES

These stuffed dates keep for at least one month. The crunchiness and saltiness of the nuts is a delightful surprise. If you have access to a grapevine the dates look lovely nestled in a box lined with leaves.

dessert dates, fresh or dried	Slit and stone.
cashews, salted	Finely chop. Pack into the dates and press to close the slit.
castor sugar	Roll the dates in until well coated.

Many years ago I lived in the beautiful old town of Dorchester in the south of England. Many of the shops were very old with bowed, mullioned windows, and were excitingly dark and mysterious inside. One such shop specialised in tobaccos, snuffs, and handmade chocolates. The scents drifting out from that shop were mouth-watering and drew you in to look and buy. My special purchase each Saturday was six stuffed chocolate dates which were very expensive and very delicious. The following two recipes are my version of that special treat.

KIRSCH AND ALMOND DATES

dessert dates	*1 box*	Slit and stone.
ground almonds	*1¼ cups*	Combine these ingredients adding
icing sugar	*1 cup*	more kirsch or icing sugar to
egg white, beaten	*1*	make a mouldable paste. Stuff the
kirsch	*2 teaspoons*	dates and press to close the slit.
compound chocolate	*180 g (6 oz)*	Melt the chocolate. Dip the dates.
white vegetable shortening	*4 teaspoons*	Place on waxed paper to set in
		the refrigerator.

GINGER BRANDIED DATES

dessert dates	*1 box*	Slit and stone.
butter	*1 tablespoon*	Melt together (see p.9).
dark chocolate	*90 g (3 oz)*	
glacé ginger	*2 tablespoons*	Add. Mix while chocolate is still
almonds, ground	*1 tablespoon*	liquid. Stuff dates. Squeeze the
rum	*2 teaspoons*	slit around the filling. Refrigerate
		for 10 minutes until firm.
compound chocolate	*180 g (6 oz)*	Melt together. Dip dates. Drain.
white vegetable shortening	*4 teaspoons*	Allow to set on waxed paper in
		the refrigerator. Pack in boxes.

CHOCOLATE BRAZIL NUTS

brazil nuts, whole	*60 g (2 oz)*	Roast (see p.11). Cool.
marzipan (see p.99)	*125 g (4 oz)*	Press firmly around the nuts to coat. Place on a rack and leave for 24 hours to dry.
compound chocolate	*125 g (4 oz)*	Melt together. Dip the coated
white vegetable shortening	*3 teaspoons*	nuts. Set on waxed paper in the refrigerator. Drizzle more chocolate thinly over to create a decorative pattern.

TURKISH DELIGHT

icing sugar, sifted castor sugar citric acid water	2 cups ½ cup 1 teaspoon 1 cup	Put in a pan. Stir over a low heat until the sugar has dissolved. Bring to boil. Cook for 10 minutes.
gelatine hot water	2 tablespoons ½ cup	Sprinkle over the water. Stir till dissolved.
rose water red food colouring	2 teaspoons as desired	Add. Stir all together. Pour into a wetted lamington tin. Leave to set in the refrigerator. Cut into squares. Roll in sieved icing sugar.

COCONUT ROUGHS

This and the following three chocolate recipes are simple and quick to make and are good to eat. Children will be able to make them (if helped) during the chocolate and shortening melting stage.

desiccated coconut	2 cups	Toast and allow to cool.
compound chocolate white vegetable shortening	250 g (8 oz) 40 g (1½ oz)	Melt. Add to coconut. Mix well. Drop teaspoonfuls on waxed paper. Refrigerate to set and store.

FRUIT AND NUT CLUSTERS

compound chocolate	220 g (7 oz)	Melt (see p.9).
dessert dates dried apricots glacé cherries crystallised ginger	¼ cup ¼ cup ¼ cup ⅛ cup	Chop all *very* finely. Mix with the chocolate. Drop teaspoonfuls on waxed paper. Set and store in the refrigerator.

CHOCOLATE GINGER

The easiest of the lot and so popular.

Dry pieces of glacé ginger in a paper towel. Melt compound chocolate. Dip the ginger. Place on waxed paper in the refrigerator to firm. Decorate with drizzled chocolate if liked.

COCONUT ICE

The ice may be covered with melted compound chocolate and cut into squares just before the chocolate is completely hard.

white vegetable shortening	*125 g (4 oz)*	Melt.
egg whites, lightly beaten vanilla essence	*2* *1 teaspoon*	Mix together in a bowl.
desiccated coconut icing sugar, sifted	*250 g (½ lb)* *500 g (1 lb)*	Add to all above. Mix well. Divide in two.
cocoa powder, sifted	*1 tablespoon*	Add to half the mixture. Mix well. Press into a 20 cm (8") square shallow container. Put the other half of the mixture on top, spread evenly, press down and smooth the top. Refrigerate till cold. Cut in squares. Keep refrigerated.

PRALINE

Praline may be eaten as a toffee or may be crushed and used as topping for desserts such as ice-creams, fruits, or custards.

almond slivers	*1 cup*	Roast (see p.11) and allow to cool in a single layer on an oiled tray.
castor sugar water	*1 cup* *4 tablespoons*	Place in a small pan over a low heat. Stir until sugar is dissolved. Increase heat and bring to a boil without stirring. Cook until golden brown, occasionally swirling the pan gently to distribute the heat. Pour over the nuts, tilting the tray if needed to spread evenly. Allow to cool and either break or crush. Store in an airtight container in the refrigerator. Use within 2 months.

MARZIPAN NUT BALLS

The marzipan may be homemade (see p.99) or bought. The soft variety of marzipan on sale is not ideal for this recipe.

made marzipan (see p.99)	*250 g (8 oz)*	Soften slightly.
pine kernels, chopped icing sugar orange liqueur	*60 g (2 oz)* *60 g (2 oz)* *1 tablespoon*	Knead into the marzipan really well. Form into little balls, about the size of a large thumbnail.
compound chocolate	*500 g (1 lb)*	Melt (see p.9). Dip the balls.
rice crispies	*375 g (12 oz)*	Roll the balls in the rice crispies before the chocolate sets. Set on waxed paper in the refrigerator and re-dip in the re-melted chocolate. Set in the refrigerator on waxed paper. Pack in airtight containers.

JAMS & MARMALADES

Kissing don't last, cookery do.
—George Meredith (1828–1909)

I have always derived a lot of satisfaction from transforming the harvest of the orchard, vegetable and herb garden into row upon row of bottles and jars on the larder shelf, the glowing colours of the fruits and vegetables promising the taste of summer on a cold, unfriendly winter day.

Jams and marmalades make an excellent present for the friend who works and has little time to make preserves but enjoys the extra flavour and goodness usually present in homemade products.

GRAPE CHEESE

black grapes	*1 kg (2 lb)*	Cook until soft. Rub through a sieve. Weigh the pulp.
lemon juice white sugar	*4 lemons* *2 cups to each* *500 g (1 lb) of pulp*	Put all with the pulp in a large pan. Stir over gentle heat until the sugar dissolves. Cook fast, stirring only occasionally for 15–20 minutes or until set (see p.11). Pour into hot sterile jars (p.11). Seal.

LEMON CURD

This preserve needs to be made in a double boiler (see p.9) or it will curdle. I like very sour curd but if this recipe is too strong for your taste you may cut down the amount of zest used. I urge you to try it first though as it is delicious. This curd keeps for a much longer time than others but it does need to be stored in the refrigerator.

unsalted butter castor sugar	*½ cup* *1 cup*	Put into a double boiler and stir over moderate heat until dissolved.
lemons	*3*	Grate the zest from all the lemons. Squeeze the juice from 2 lemons and add to the pan.
large eggs	*3*	Beat and strain the eggs. Pour into the pan. Cook, stirring occasionally, until thick enough to coat the back of a wooden spoon. *Don't allow the mixture to boil or get too hot.* The curd will thicken more as it cools. Pour into hot, sterile jars. Seal.

PASSIONFRUIT BUTTER

Those of you with access to a passionfruit vine will be able to make lots of this wonderful butter. Tinned passionfruit makes a good substitute for fresh. I dislike eating pips or seeds so I sieve the butter before putting in the jars. This isn't necessary if the seeds don't bother you.

passionfruit, large	*12*	Scoop the flesh from the shells.

citric acid	1 teaspoon	Mix all together. Put in a double boiler (see p.9). Stir over moderate heat until the sugar is dissolved and the butter has melted. Continue to cook until the butter is thick enough to coat the back of a wooden spoon. Press through a sieve if you want to remove the seeds. Pour into clean warm jars. Seal.
white sugar	2 cups	
butter	2 tablespoons	
eggs, beaten, strained	4	

PEAR MARMALADE

lemons	1	Peel thinly. Squeeze juice. Save pips and tie in a muslin bag. Slice the peel into very thin strips. Soak the bag of pips and the peel in water for 24 hours. Drain.
oranges	1	
firm pears, peeled, diced	1 kg (2 lb)	Put all in a large strong pan. Simmer until the pears are tender—about 10-15 minutes.
water	½ cup	
fresh ginger root, crushed	1 tablespoon	
white sugar, warmed	2 cups	Pour in. Stir on a low heat until the sugar is dissolved. Bring to a rolling boil until a set (p.11) is obtained—about 10-15 minutes. Pour into warm, sterile jars.

HERB JELLY

Serve with cold meats, pies, cheeses.

cooking apples, chopped	1 kg (2 lb)	Put in a non-aluminium pan with enough water to just cover. Cook till soft. Drip overnight in a jelly bag (see p.11).
white sugar	500 g (1 lb) to 500 ml (2 cups) juice	Measure juice. Heat the sugar with the juice until dissolved.
lemon juice	1 lemon	Tie the herbs in a muslin bag and add all to the pan. Bring to boiling point and simmer until a set is achieved (see p.11). Remove bag. Ladle into hot sterile pots. Cool slightly. Add sprigs of fresh, clean, dry herbs. Seal.
cider vinegar	¼ cup	
fresh herbs, chopped	30 g (1 oz)	

MANDARIN OR TANGERINE MARMALADE

These two fruits are so closely related that I can't tell the difference. In Britain there used to be only tangerines and here in Australia the mandarin is the one available.

   The smell of mandarins takes me back in time to the Christmases of my childhood. Waking in the dark to feel a heavy, lumpy stocking at the end of my bed and to know that 'he' had been. In the toe of the treasure-filled stocking there was always a shiny new sixpence and a tangerine. I still find the smell as exciting as I did those many years ago.

mandarins lemons	500 g (1 lb) 250 g (8 oz)	Peel thinly, remove and save pips and squeeze the juice out. Tie the pips in a piece of muslin. Shred the peel *very* thinly.
water	7 cups	Put in a strong pan with all the above (including the bag of pips). Simmer for 1½ hours. Remove the pips, squeezing the bag well to get all the juice back into the pan.
sugar, warmed	6 cups	Add. Stir over a low heat until dissolved. Bring to a rolling boil until a setting point is reached (p.11). See p.11 for tips on dealing with scum. Cool slightly.
brandy	2 tablespoons	Add. Stir. Pot.

RED CAPSICUM JELLY

A most attractive red jelly which is wonderful eaten with hot or cold meats or cheese and crusty brown bread.

   See p.9 for hints on dealing with chillies.

red peppers, chopped, seeded red chillies, chopped, seeded cider vinegar	4 cups ½ cup 2½ cups	Simmer together for 30 minutes. Drip overnight in a jelly-bag (see p.11). Don't be tempted to squeeze the bag. Put liquid in a strong, non-aluminium pan.
white sugar salt	7 cups ¾ teaspoon	Add, stir well to dissolve sugar. Bring slowly to a boil. Boil hard for one minute. Remove from heat.
pectin	1 bottle	Add, deal with scum (see p.11). Pour into hot jars. Seal.

APRICOT AND COINTREAU CONSERVE

I love fresh apricots but the season for this fruit is fairly short, so by making this conserve with dried apricots I am able to enjoy the delicious intensity of the fruit year-round. Anyone would appreciate a pot of this wonderful sun-coloured conserve.

dried apricots water	500 g (1 lb) 6 cups	Quarter the apricots. Add the water. Cover and soak for 2 days. Stir occasionally.
orange lemon	1 1	Peel, leaving no white pith on the rinds. Slice finely. Soak overnight in cold water. Drain.
sugar, white	6 cups	Warm and put into a large preserving pan with all the above.
lemon juice	2 lemons	Add. Heat, stirring until sugar is dissolved. Bring to a boil. Cook until set (see p.11).
Cointreau or kirsch	4 tablespoons	Add and stir. Pour into hot, sterile jars. Seal when cold.

LIME AND GINGER MARMALADE

This marmalade is nicest if limes are used but you can still make a wonderful marmalade using lemons instead. Limes are very high in pectin so the seeds don't need to be used to aid setting. However if you substitute lemons you should tie the seeds in a muslin bag and cook these with the fruit.

limes	1 kg (2 lb)	Slice very finely. Discard seeds. Put into a large basin.
water	8 cups	Pour over the fruit. Stand overnight. Next day, pour into a large pan, bring to boil and simmer, covered, for 1½ hours or until the rind is tender.
white sugar, warmed root ginger, crushed	7 cups 1 tablespoon	Tie the ginger in a muslin bag. Add all. Stir over moderate heat until sugar is dissolved. Bring to a full rolling boil and cook, without stirring, for about 20 minutes or until a set is achieved (see p.11). Remove muslin bag.
brandy preserved ginger, chopped	¼ cup ½ cup	Add. Stand for about 10 minutes. Stir, then pour into warm sterile pots. Cool and seal.

PEANUT PASTE

There are several advantages in making your own nut pastes: freshness, desired texture, and lack of additives. Almond, cashew and hazelnut butters can be made using the same method.

raw, blanched peanuts	*500 g (1 lb)*	Roat (see p.11). Cool.
salt (optional) peanut oil	*½ teaspoon* *⅓ cup*	Put ⅓ of the nuts in a blender with the salt. Start blending. Drizzle the oil in until smooth. Add more peanuts and more oil until the paste is as fine or crunchy as you like.

DRINKS OF ALL SORTS

I drink only to make my friends seem interesting.
—Don Marquis (1878–1937)

PASSIONFRUIT CORDIAL

To serve, dilute with water or mineral water and add ice. Keep refrigerated. The cordials will keep for three weeks.

passionfruit	12	Spoon the pulp into a large bowl.
lemons	3	Add the juice and grate the yellow rind (no white).
white sugar water	3 cups 3 cups	Stir over a low heat until the sugar is dissolved. Increase heat. Boil for 10 minutes.
tartaric acid	2 teaspoons	Add. Stir to dissolve. Pour over fruit. Stand, covered, for 24 hours. Strain and bottle.

LEMON CORDIAL

I like to add a sprig or two of peppermint and a few slices of lemon to a jug of this cordial.

lemons	6	Grate the rind (no white) and squeeze the juice. Put in a large bowl.
boiling water	8 cups	Pour over.
white sugar citric acid Epsom salts	8 cups 5 tablespoons 2 tablespoons	Add. Mix well. Stand for 24 hours. Strain. Bottle. Keep refrigerated.

GINGER BEER PLANT

Ginger beer can become very alcoholic. A good friends of mine saved the beer for her son's party so that each guest could have his own bottle. An hour after the party began I had a tearful 'phone call: 14 little boys seemed hell-bent on wrecking her house and were totally out of control—should she 'phone the parents, and tell them that their 10-year-old boys were drunk, or say nothing and wait for the alcohol to wear off? She chose the former course, saved her home from ruin, and served lemon cordial at the next party.

lemons	1	Pour all the juice and one teaspoon of the pulp into a large jar with a well-fitting top.

OPPOSITE
Grandma's basket might include date and walnut loaf, a box of mixed biscuits, passionfruit butter, pickles and rollmops, and a selection of sweets (see also p.133).
OVERLEAF
A vegetarian basket might include mushroom pâté, pickles, soya sunnies, apricot slices, yesame powder, curried almonds, herb mustard, honeyed herb vinegar, anise liqueur, chocolates.

baker's yeast	60 g (2 oz)	Crumble into the jar.
ground ginger white sugar water	2 teaspoons 2 teaspoons 1¼ cups	Add. Stir and fasten the lid loosely.

Feeding:
Feed each day with one teaspoon sugar and one teaspoon ground ginger.

To make the ginger beer:
Strain the plant through cheesecloth. Squeeze well. Retain both the liquid and the residue.

You will need strong bottles such as beer bottles and patent seal caps or corks tied down with string. *Never* use screw tops, as the bottles may burst.

sugar boiling water lemon juice	2 cups 5 cups 25 lemons	Mix together in a large bowl. Add the liquid from the plant. Stir until the sugar is dissolved.
water	4.5 L (8 pints)	Add. Bottle and seal. Leave for 5 days in a cool place before drinking.

To restart the plant:
Divide the residue in half. Put one-half in the jar, add 1¼ cups of water and feed as before. The remaining half may be given away or discarded.

GINGER BEER 2

lemons	2	Put the yellow peel (no pith) and juice into a large bowl. Save the squeezed lemons.
sugar root ginger, crushed	1 kg (2 lb) 45 g (1½ oz)	Add.
water	4 L (8 pints, approx.)	Bring to a boil with the squeezed lemons. Pour into the bowl. Remove the lemon. Stir to dissolve sugar. Cover and leave to cool to blood heat.
dried, granulated yeast	1 teaspoon	Dissolve in a little of the warm liquid. Leave 30 minutes. Add to the bowl.
cream of tartar	¼ teaspoon	Stir in. Cover. Leave for 24 hours before straining and bottling. The same precautions apply as for the previous ginger beer recipe.

ALDO'S MAMMA'S CAPPUCCINO

For those who adore fluffy, delicious coffee but don't own a cappuccino machine, here is a really interesting recipe. It will keep well without separating for about one week, but can be restored at any time by beating. It is only for those who take sugar with coffee, as it doesn't work without it.

Use 1 heaped teaspoonful of the paste to a cup of near-boiling water (boiling water should never be used for coffee, as it destroys some of the flavour). I haven't met Aldo or his mamma but I thank them and the friend who passed this recipe to me.

instant coffee	6 tablespoons	Beat with a rotary beater until
raw sugar	6 tablespoons	*very* stiff and creamy. The mixture
cold water	3 tablespoons (scant)	should be the colour of milk chocolate. Store in the refrigerator.

Teas

Tea, although an Oriental, is a gentleman at least;
Cocoa is a cad and a coward, cocoa is a vulgar beast.
—G.K. Chesterton (1874–1936)

CHAI

When I first went to Poona in India I had great difficulty getting what I thought of as a 'decent cup of tea', as the Indian version, 'chai', was very different. After my initial resistance I became very fond of this exotic tea. For lovers of this drink you could give packets of the dry mixture in a jar or tin with instructions for making attached.

root ginger, sliced dried	4 tablespoons	Mix well. Divide the mixture in 4
cinnamon sticks, broken	8	and package in small bags.
cloves, whole	32	
peppercorns, whole	32	
cardamom seeds	16	
tea bags	3 to each spice packet	

To make:
Put the contents of one packet in a pan with 4 cups of water. Bring to the boil and simmer for 10 minutes. Add the 3 teabags and 2½ cups of milk. Bring to the boil again. Turn the heat off. Cover and stand for two minutes. Strain, and sweeten to taste.

CHINESE LEMON TEA

Light, refreshing, and very green. This tea would make a lovely gift accompanied by either a beautiful teapot or a fine porcelain cup and saucer.

Chinese green tea	*250 g*	
lemon verbena leaves	*handful*	Dry and crumble to a tea-like texture. Add to the tea. Package in small bags.
lemon grass leaves	*4 leaves*	
peppermint leaves	*small handful*	

To make:
Add to a warmed teapot in the same amounts as you would use for ordinary tea. Allow to brew. Sweeten with honey. Don't add milk.

SUMMER TEA

cinnamon sticks	*4*	Grind or crush coarsely. *Not* to a powder.
whole cloves	*40*	
orange rind, dried	*4 oranges, no pith*	
lemon rind, dried	*4 lemons, no pith*	
tea leaves	*¾ cup*	Add. Divide into 8. Pack in small paper or cheesecloth bags and then in a jar or tin.

To make:
Empty one bag into a warmed teapot. Pour three cups of boiling water over. Steep for 3 minutes, strain. Sweeten with honey. This tea is better if drunk without milk.

'LOVING CUP' TEA

This is a comforting tea to drink on a cold winter night. Dried hibiscus flowers are available from health food stores.

cinnamon sticks, crumbled	*4*	Mix all well. Spread out on a tray in a warm place for two days to dry. Stir often. Store in an airtight container.
orange peel, grated (no pith)	*2 oranges*	
lemon peel, grated (no pith)	*1 lemon*	
cloves, crushed	*1 teaspoon*	
aniseed, crushed	*1 teaspoon*	
nutmeg, ground	*½ teaspoon*	
black peppercorns, crushed	*⅛ teaspoon*	
hibiscus flowers, dried, crushed	*60 g (2 oz)*	

To make:
Make as conventional tea, use honey to sweeten. This tea is better if drunk without milk.

Wines and Liqueurs

Candy is dandy but liquor is quicker.

—Ogden Nash

These alcoholic drinks range from healthy herbal wines (nonetheless delicious) to frankly decadent liqueurs.

ROSEMARY DIGESTIVE WINE

One of the soothers for stomachs which have been 'overindulged'. Sip a glass of this wine after dinner to combat indigestion.

dry white wine	1 bottle	Heat together to blood heat in a
honey	2 tablespoons	non-aluminium pan. Stir to dissolve the honey.
orange peel	1 orange	Bruise gently. Put in a large jar.
fennel seeds	1 teaspoon	Pour the warm wine over. Seal.
rosemary	6 cm sprig	Shake daily for one week. Strain and filter.
brandy	150 ml	Add. Re-bottle. Leave 2 weeks before using.

MULLED WINE

I have magical memories of winter nights at our farm, 'Rivendell'. Firelight flickering, the company of good friends, and a guitar being softly played. Fragrant, steaming glasses of mulled wine warmed us from within as the wind howled up the valley and buffeted the walls and windows. Mulled wine is an inexpensive gift which will be remembered by the recipients for a long time, especially if given in the winter.

lemon peel, dried, ground	½ teaspoon	Combine and fasten in a
cinnamon stick, crushed	½	cheesecloth bag.
whole cloves, bruised	4	
coriander seeds, bruised	4	
nutmeg, ground	1 teaspoon	
white sugar	1 tablespoon	
claret	1 bottle	Tie the bag to the neck of the bottle. Attach a card with instructions as follows:

Pour the claret and the contents of the bag into a non-aluminium pan. Heat gently and very slowly. Don't allow to boil. Strain. Pour into heatproof glasses and enjoy!

THIRTEEN-HERB LIQUEUR

This is a very fine semi-dry digestive liqueur to serve to your friends when they have overindulged at your table.

sage leaves	3	Chop the herbs coarsely. Bruise the spices. Put all in a large jar with a well-fitting lid.
wormwood leaflets	10	
lemon leaves	6	
lemon balm leaves	6	
bay leaves	2	
rosemary leaves	10	
caraway seeds	1 teaspoon	
chamomile flowers	¼ teaspoon	
peppermint leaves	10	
dandelion root, crushed	1 teaspoon	
coriander seeds	6	
cinnamon stick, broken	1 cm (½″)	
cloves, whole	3	
vodka	1 cup	Add to the jar. Leave for 2 weeks, shaking the jar daily. Strain through filter paper. Return to the jar.
dry white vermouth	2 cups	
sugar	1–2 cups	Add to the jar. Cover. Stand for a further 2 weeks, shaking daily. Re-strain. Bottle and seal. Store in a cool, dark place for 3 months before drinking.

ANISE LIQUEUR

This is my favourite liqueur as the flavour of the seeds is reminiscent of liquorice which I love. These seeds are all digestives so this is another good liqueur to drink after a heavy or rich meal.

caraway seeds	1 tablespoon	Bruise the seeds lightly. Put in a large jar with a well-fitting lid.
fennel seeds	1 teaspoon	
aniseed	1 teaspoon	
coriander	30 seeds	
cloves	4	
white sugar	1 cup	Pour over the seeds. Leave for 2 weeks, shaking daily. Strain through filter paper into bottles. Seal corks with wax. Mature quietly in a dark place for 4 months.
vodka	3 cups	

MANDARIN BRANDY

Most people love the flavour and aroma of mandarins. This is a really beautiful after-dinner drink, golden, and sweetly perfumed.

mandarins, quartered	6	Put all into a large jar with a well-fitting lid. Shake the jar daily for one month to dissolve the sugar. Strain through filter paper. Bottle. Seal corks with wax. Store in a cool, dark place for 6 months before using.
brandy	4 cups	
sugar	1 cup	

LEMON LIQUEUR

We once made a large cask of this liqueur as it is a favourite among our friends. The cask was left to mature on the wooden floor of the larder but it developed a leak and the very potent brew dripped through the floorboards to the ground underneath the house. Here it was discovered and sampled by our chickens, who staggered around helplessly but contentedly for several hours.

If a sweeter liqueur is liked the amount of sugar may be increased.

lemons	6	Peel thinly. Don't use *any* pith. Chop finely. Put in a large jar with a well-fitting lid.
cinnamon stick, crumbled	2.5 cm (1")	Add to the jar. Fasten lid. Leave for 4 weeks in a cool, dark place. Shake daily to dissolve sugar. Strain through filter paper. Bottle. Seal corks with wax. Store in a cool, dark place for 4 months before using.
coriander seeds, crushed	20	
sugar	1 cup	
brandy	4 cups	

STRAWBERRY LIQUEUR

strawberries, hulled, sliced	1 kg (2 lb)	Put all into a large jar with a well-fitting lid. Leave in a cool, dark place for one week, shaking daily to dissolve sugar. Strain through filter paper. Bottle, cork. Leave 2 months to mature before drinking.
gin or vodka	3 cups	
sugar	2 cups	

COFFEE LIQUEUR 1

One of the most popular after-dinner drinks, this recipe is easy to make and will be a very welcome gift.

Use a good quality coffee or the finished result will be disappointing.

instant coffee powder	90 g (3 oz)	Dissolve together over a low heat. Don't boil. Allow to cool completely. Put in a large jar with a well-fitting lid.
boiling water	2 cups	
white sugar	2 cups	
brandy	4 cups	Add to the jar. Cover. Leave for one week in a cool, dark place. Strain through filter paper into bottles. Leave for 4 months before drinking.
lemon peel (*no* pith)	1 lemon	
vanilla pod, bruised	2.5 cm (1")	

COFFEE LIQUEUR 2

water	1½ cups	Stir over a low heat until the sugar is dissolved. Bring to boil. Simmer for 3 minutes. Cool.
instant coffee powder	60 g (2 oz)	
sugar	1½ cups	
vanilla essence	3 teaspoons	Add. Strain through filter paper. Bottle, cork. Store in a cool, dark place for 4 months before drinking.
brandy	2 cups	
rum	4 tablespoons	

RASPBERRY GIN

This is a richly coloured and flavoured liqueur. Serve it in tall glasses over crushed ice or with tonic.

gin or vodka	1 bottle	Empty the gin into a very clean jug. Crush the berries and push into the bottle.
raspberries	500 g (1 lb)	
sugar	1½ cups	Add. Top up with gin. Reserve remaining gin in a clean bottle. Shake several times a day for one week or so to dissolve the sugar. Store in a cool, dark place for 6 months before straining through double cheesecloth and then filter paper. Re-bottle. Top up with the reserve gin and store a further 3 months before drinking.
cloves	4	

Packaging

The range of packaging you will need includes: containers such as jars and bottles, labels, both swing and stick-on gift cards, boxes, and paper. In these days of awareness of the need to conserve our resources wherever possible we can use all sorts of recycled materials for our packaging. Old greetings cards may have the plain parts cut away to make swing tags, bottles and jars can be washed and re-used, and newspaper may be turned into original wrapping paper (not directly next to food though).

If you intend to make a large number of gifts it is advisable to have a cupboard for storage of boxes, jars, cards, paints, and craft materials. There is a degree of frustration in having to hunt in many places before you can begin a project. Try to put part of a weekend aside initially to concentrate on making a small stockpile of papers and labels. If you wait until a gift is due you might not have time to make the packaging and so end up buying it. I try to devote at least a couple of hours to making wrapping paper and make several different types at a time so that I have paper for all occasions. I have a little bag which has lead pencils, coloured pencils, felt-tipped pens, a pair of scissors, several blank labels, and gift cards; this bag is ready to be picked up and used if I have five minutes to spare, talking to friends, waiting for something to cook on the stove or on a picnic. You need not be an artist to create a lovely card; sometimes the simplest design is the most effective, or you can trace a design or picture and colour it in yourself. Once you begin, you will get inspiration from many sources.

Jars and Bottles

Recycled jars or bottles should be washed in hot soapy water and put upside down in a warm oven to sterilise. Replace the lids before you store the jars, to keep the insides clean. The jars and bottles may have unattractive lids which can be painted in colours to match the contents, can be covered with material, or can be covered with a paper doily. Use an elastic band over material covers before tying ribbon around the necks of jars, as this makes the ribbon easier to tie and looks professional.

Labels and Gift Cards

The following pages have patterns of labels that you can copy or trace. The sizes are suitable for swing tags and stick-on labels but if you want them larger or smaller they may be photocopied, enlarged or reduced, directly onto a sheet of white gummed paper which is easy to buy from office suppliers. Your labels may be left black and white (sometimes this is very effective), coloured with felt tipped pen, or painted or filled in with crayon. I have gold and silver fine-point markers which I use a lot. I've never had much success with the felt-tipped variety but the fine metal-tipped ones are easy and fun to use, giving a professional appearance to the card. Another interesting thing to use on the labels is fabric paint of the type which dries raised from the paper. This paint can give dimension and interest to an otherwise rather boring label.

Experiment with different weights of card or paper. I like a good quality, quite thick watercolour paper best both for tags and greeting cards. I sometimes buy expensive paper but I get dozens of cards and labels from one sheet. I also ask my local printers for card and paper offcuts which cost nothing and are frequently top quality. Make sure however that the ink isn't going to 'bleed' on your chosen paper. A good art suppliers' shop will be able to guide you in this matter.

Some of the labels may be copied onto folded thin card, and instructions, a greeting, or recipe may be written on the rear portion.

Enlarged, some of the labels would be suitable for greetings cards to go with your gift. Dried pressed fern fronds, grasses, and small flowers can be stuck on the cards in the central plain portion to make beautiful and original greetings cards. It's a good idea to make greetings and gift cards at the same time as making the paper. Lay the card next to the paper and spray or stipple to make a matching set.

Paper for Gift-wrapping

There are several types of paper suitable for wrapping gifts: butchers', tissue, cellophane, newspaper, plain paper which you have decorated, crêpe paper and serviettes. I also save all wrapping paper I have received, iron it and re-use it. Below are some ideas for decorating your own paper.

LACE PAPER

This is easy to do and is pretty. You will need:
  newspaper
  plain wrapping paper or cellophane
  cans of spray enamel
  pieces of lace curtains with reasonably bold patterns

Method
Lay newspaper on a garden table or other firm surface out of doors. Place a piece of paper or cellophane on top and lay the lace over the paper. Smooth the lace as close to the paper as possible. Spray evenly with one or two colours. Lift the lace away from the paper and hang the paper on the clothes line to dry.

FERN PAPER

Using the same method as above, lay the fern fronds or other flat leaves on the paper, cover with fly-screening, and spray.

STIPPLED PAPER

I found a large coarse sponge on the beach, cut it in half and now use it for 'stippling' paper. It gives an interesting, uneven design. Any sponge may be used but if it is too fine there is not enough definition. You will need:
  sponge
  poster or acrylic paints
  paper (butchers' paper will do)
  two dinner plates
  board
  drawing pins

Method
Pin the paper to the board. Mix the paint to a very thin cream consistency and pour onto the plate. Two colours are usually sufficient. Dip the sponge into the paint, shake off the surplus and dab the paint onto the paper. Repeat with the second colour.
  You could try using screwed-up foil, string, straw matting or anything with texture, instead of the sponge. Leave the paper to dry before removing it from the board.

STENCILLING

Stencilled paper can look professional and is easy and inexpensive to make. Use simple designs as these are quicker to do and are more effective than very complex ones. In addition to paper the following will be needed, all available from art suppliers:

acetate
acrylic paints
stencil brush or fine sponge
ballpoint pen for drawing designs
cutting knife
tracing paper
pencil
piece of glass or wood to cut on

Method
Tape your traced design to the piece of glass or wood. Lay the acetate sheet over the design. Cut the stencil. Lay the stencil on the paper and colour in using the stencil brush and acrylic paint.

MARBLED PAPER

Use thin cartridge paper for this effect. If the paper is too absorbent the paint soaks up before it 'marbles'. Wear old clothes and make the paper in a garden shed or out of doors where the mess won't matter. You will need:
cartridge paper
old baking tray (not too deep)
oil-based enamels
vinegar

Method
Fill the tray with water, add two tablespoons of vinegar. Stir. Drip one or two colours and swirl gently using a wide-toothed comb or a stick. Pull the paper over the surface of the water, keeping the baking try very still and the water in total contact with the paper. Hang on a line to dry. Clean the surface of the water with newspaper or paper towelling.

STAMPED PAPER

An interesting effect can be achieved by stamping paper with objects dipped in acrylic paint. All sorts of objects of different textures and shapes can be used as stamps; for example:
sweet capsicum sliced in half and dried
foil crumpled-up
honan matting
string glued onto card in a decorative pattern

FABRIC PAINT PAPER

There are many varieties of fabric paint on the market, some of which have a raised look when dry. I use these paints most effectively on tissue and cellophane paper. Dot simple designs of flowers, stars, circles and other shapes on the paper in one or two colours. Allow to dry flat.

FLYSCREEN STENCILS

This is another simple method which children find fun to do.

Lay leaves of distinctive patterns all over the paper. Lay a piece of flyscreen mesh on top of the leaves and, using a broad house-painting brush and either diluted water or acrylic paints, paint over the flyscreen.

CREATIVE WRAPPINGS

In these days when we are so aware of conservation you might wish to avoid using paper at all. In this case, a plain or printed tea-towel, pretty scarf or handkerchief makes an additional gift and saves paper.

Boxes

BOXES 1, 2, 3

Card for making boxes needs to be strong enough to support the contents but also thin enough to fold. Plain card can be covered with patterned paper or may be decorated using any of the paper decorating techniques. All decorating needs to be done before the box is made up.

Box pattern 1

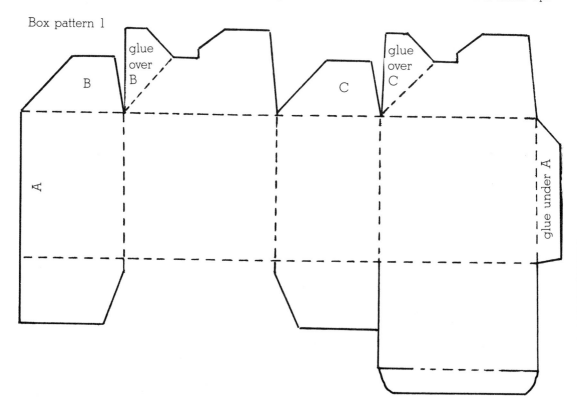

Patterns are given for three boxes which are easy to make and one which, even though more complex, is so beautiful that I have included it. Two of the boxes require little gluing, and the flat chocolate box requires no glue at all. Where gluing is needed, a craft glue or double-sized sticky tape may be used. These boxes will stay shut without any further fastening but the box can be further decorated with ribbons if you like.

As these box patterns have been reduced to fit the pages of this book, you will need to enlarge them (this can be done easily by means of a photocopier). Place a sheet of carbon paper between the enlarged pattern and the card, and trace around the edges of the pattern to transfer it to the card.

All solid lines indicate cutting lines. All broken lines indicate folds. Use the back of a knife blade on the back of the design to score the broken lines.

Box pattern 2

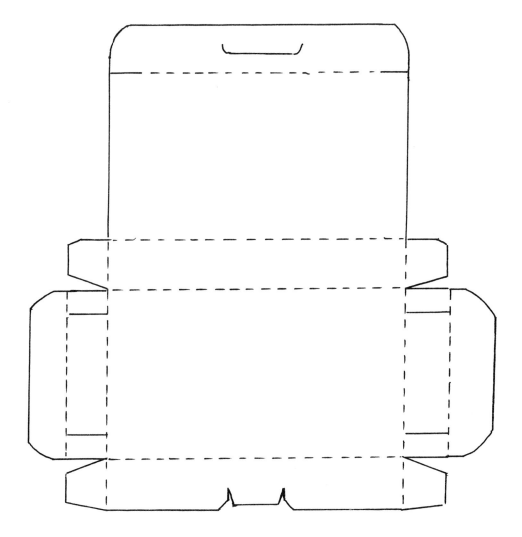

Box pattern 3

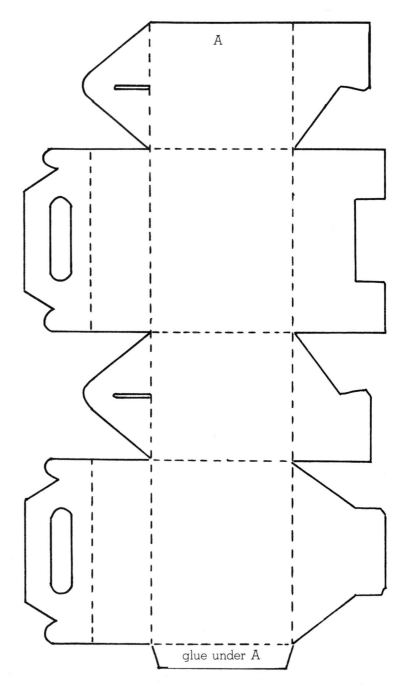

A

glue under A

OPPOSITE
A wine and cheese basket might include yoghurt cheese balls, crackers, lemon olives, marinated capsicum salad, apricot jellies, mulled wine, and herb liqueur (see also p.134).

BOX 4 'THE LOTUS'

All the folds in this pattern must be made after cutting out and *before* gluing. All folds must be very sharp to give this box its special appearance. The box is symmetrical, so the folds need to be as accurate as possible.

The 'tag' at the bottom of the box is fed through all the slots and then bent over or glued for extra strength.

All *A* creases fold to the *inside* of the box. All *B* creases fold to the *outside* of the box.

To close the box, fold the flower petals as shown and push down gently. The flower will then hold the box firmly shut. (See p.130 for finished views of top and base.)

Box pattern 4

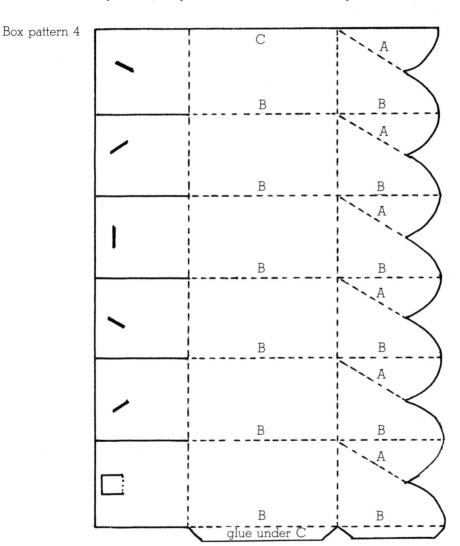

OPPOSITE
A housewarming basket might include marinated fetta, brandied tomatoes, peppercorn mustard, and a selection of pickles, oils and wines.

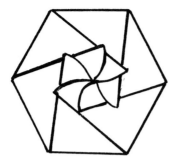

Finished view of top

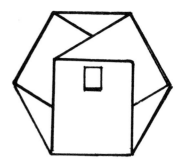

Finished view of base

To expand your range of boxes, the contents of the grocery cupboard will probably be a source of inspiration. Find a box which appeals to you, open it out flat, lay it on a piece of thin cartridge paper and draw round it very carefully. Transfer to your card in the same way as described above. All box patterns may easily be changed in proportion to suit the contents.

If the contents of the box are greasy or sticky you may like to line the inside with a paper doily or other paper before filling.

An effective, quick and festive type of packaging goodies is to make a paper cracker. Put the sweets, chocolates, or biscuits in a long cellophane bag (the size of this parcel determines the size of the cracker). To form the tube, cut a piece of thin cardboard to the size needed to enclose the contents. Cut an outside wrapper of decorative paper which is three times longer and 5 cm (2") wider than the cardboard. Place the cardboard and the cellophane bag in the centre of the paper and roll to enclose neatly. Fasten with a piece of transparent sticky tape. Fasten the ends with elastic bands and decorate with ribbons, bows, or tinsel.

Baskets

'Yes,' said Pooh. 'We had breakfast together yesterday. By the Pine Trees.
I'd made up a little basket, just a little, fair sized basket, an ordinary biggish sort of basket, full of—'. . .

—A.A. Milne (1882–1956)

The concept of giving a basket (or other container) is to present a complete package, of the type which you can afford, beautifully hand-labelled and gift-tagged with boxes and paper lovingly made by you. Very few of the recipes in this book are expensive to make, so the entire gift may cost very little money but it will be admired and appreciated in a way that no shop-bought article is likely to be.

Baskets don't need to be new. Second-hand shops, barter markets, garage and boot sales are some of the places to pick up basket bargains. Scrub the basket thoroughly and paint it if it's shabby. The idea is to give a gift which is original, affordable, useful and exciting—what more could you ask!

The baskets or containers could be lined with tissue paper, shredded cellophane, paper napkins, a tea-towel, or a tablecloth. If it is a very beautiful basket, do not decorate it at all. I never feel it necessary to wrap a basket unless it's very small but I try to colour co-ordinate the contents for the best visual impact. The handle of the basket could have a ribbon, a bow, some tinsel or a small bunch of dried flowers attached to it. The lids of bottles and jars should be sealed with tape if there is any chance of the contents leaking into the basket.

The food suggested in the baskets below is not a comprehensive list of the recipes in this book, but merely ideas to start you off. You will think of many more baskets of your own as occasions arise. Some of these might be weddings, housewarmings, camping trips, children's birthdays and so on.

Below, you will find some suggestions for gifts to put in the baskets but you will be guided by your knowledge of the recipient—after all, there are people who like to drink wine and eat pâté for breakfast!

THE BREAKFAST BASKET

This basket could be lined with a checked cloth and could include fresh eggs, and egg cups. The cloth could be tied in a knot over the contents. Some suitable contents would be:
    golden granola
    lemon curd
    mandarin marmalade to eat with pikelets
    herb cheese pot with crackers
    tea mix

THE LUNCH BASKET

Hem a piece of sprigged material to double as a basket-liner and tablecloth. If the basket is to be used the day it is received you could include a ripe avocado and a crusty French loaf to complement the other foods. Include some of the following to create an exciting lunch:
    pâté, potted cheese and crackers
    marinated vegetables
    rollmops
    fruit in brandy
    a bottle of rosemary wine to round off the meal

THE TEA-TIME BASKET

Instead of a basket you could buy a small tea-tray and tray cloth. Lay the gifts on the tray, cover the whole with clear cellophane and decorate with ribbons. Some of the following would be suitable contents and a beautiful cup and saucer or teapot would make the gift very special:
    almond ricciarelli
    macaroons
    gingerbread
    pikelet mix
    passionfruit butter
    tea mix

THE DINNER BASKET

If you want to give just a few items for this gift, the container could be a casserole holding:
   pâté
   crackers
   a jar of pesto
   a packet of pasta
   a few chocolate Brazil nuts or chocolate ginger

If you are giving a basket you could line it with two linen napkins and include:
   vinaigrette
   brandied fruit salad
   a bottle of caraway liqueur
The basket would be lovely if lined with two linen napkins, and a couple of candles would ensure a romantic dinner.

THE AFTER-DINNER BASKET

It's possible to buy wine-decanting baskets inexpensively. A choice of one of the liqueurs or wines with a box of chocolates nestling to the side would make the recipient very happy. You could also include a set of liqueur glasses. Other ideas could be prunes in brandy and a selection from the nuts, with a dish to serve them in.

THE PICNIC BASKET

A fitted-out picnic basket with a selection of suitable foods would make a terrific present if you can afford it. Otherwise a smaller basket containing a few of the items and tied up in a bright checked tablecloth would be appreciated just as much. Choose from:
   marinated fetta
   potted cheese
   crackers
   rollmops
   spiced cherries
   spicy peps
   gingerbread

THE CAKE-MAKER'S BASKET

Keen cake-makers are always looking for unusual cake tins. I have a huge heart-shaped tin which is used for family birthdays, anniversaries, and other occasions. Try to find a large, interesting tin, and pack it with some of the following items:

vanilla essence
ginger root in sherry
lemon curd
candied peel
dried citrus powder
crystallised flowers

Additional gifts could include a bamboo ginger grater, a waterproof apron, a granite pestle and mortar. The whole thing could be tied up in a bright tea-towel knotted on top.

THE GOURMET COOK'S BASKET

Here is another opportunity for an unusual container. A huge and handsome mixing bowl, an earthenware chicken pot or a ceramic casserole would all be suitable for holding a selection of wonderful gifts. Choose from:

vinegars
herbs and spices
pickled lemons
cheese sauce
ginger root or horseradish root in sherry
selection of oils
pesto
pickled nasturtium seeds
one of the curry powders

A bunch or posy of fresh herbs tied with a long ribbon would look delightful to 'dress up' the gift.

GRANDMA'S BASKET

Make this basket as pretty as you possibly can, line it with broderie anglaise or similar material, fasten ribbon or bows to the handle and fill it with things which your grandmother will enjoy. Some of the items might take her on a trip down memory lane to her childhood. Choose from delicacies such as:

farmhouse potted cheese
herbal tonic wine
Sylvia's date and apple chutney
chocolate truffles
macaroons
rollmops
a packet of summer tea

You may like to include a bone-china cup and saucer, a little teapot, or a rose holder. A fresh rosebud would look lovely tied to the basket.

THE VEGETARIAN BASKET

Your vegetarian friend may be a lover of all things natural. Try to find a basket woven from interesting materials. I have a very beautiful one made from pine needles held together with flax. Another choice of container could be an earthenware planter or cooking pot. Fill the basket or pot with some of the following goodies:
mushroom pâté
pesto
marinated vegetables
brandied tomatoes
golden granola
yesame powder
herb salt
potted cheese
mixed mint liqueur
A handmade mug, soup or cereal bowl are special extra gifts.

THE WINE AND CHEESE BASKET

If this is for friends who entertain a lot, a tray might be appropriate instead of a basket. However if you want to use a basket, you could choose a flat 'trug' shape which could be used afterwards for bread rolls, cheee and biscuits, or fruit. I like to use shredded coloured cellophane in the basket; dark red looks both sophisticated and festive. Some suggestions are:
rosemary wine
mandarin liqueur
marinated olives
marinated mushrooms
curried nuts
crackers
a selection of cheeses
Additional gifts such as a set of wine glasses, large paper napkins or toothpicks in a holder would be appreciated.

THE 'CHRISTMAS FOR TWO' BASKET

This is the easiest basket to decorate. Use tinsel, baubles, and red paper. Tiny inflated balloons tied to the handle of the basket are colourful and bright. Choose from:
pâté and crackers
little Christmas cakes
hazelnut truffles
stuffed dates
ricciarelli
almond shortbreads
devilled nuts
a bottle of anise liqueur
The addition of party hats, balloons, and crackers make this a fun basket to give and receive.

Index

ABSNRIC